HOOLIGANISM

BY
MIKE HOULIHAN

Cover design by Ryan Norris
Photo by John Karl Breun

First published by Dog Ear Publishing
4010 W. 86th Street, Ste H
Indianapolis, IN 46268
www.dogearpublishing.net

dog ear
PUBLISHING

ISBN: 978-159858-725-8

This book is printed on acid-free paper.

Printed in the United States of America

Chicago Tribune

FOUNDED June 10. 1847

JOHN W. MADIGAN, *President and Publisher*   JACK FULLER. *Editor*

LOIS WILLE. *Editorial Page Editor*   COLLEEN DISHON, *Associate Editor*   F. RICHARD CICCONE, *Managing Editor*
N. DON WYCLIFF. *Deputy Editorial Page Editor*   DOUGLAS E. KNEELAND. *Associate Editor*   DENIS GOSSELIN, *Associate Editor*

Voice of the people

Time to give the Hooligans a break

EVANSTON—In the wake of probably one of the most vociferous political campaigns in Chicago history, I would like to raise my voice in alarm regarding a form of media prejudice that continually slanders my good name.

In his column recently reporting on the shootings that took place among supporters of Cook County sheriff's candidates O'Grady and Sheahan, Mike Royko referred to the perpetrators as "hooligans." Hooligan is an ancient Irish derivation of my name, Houlihan, and I am sick and tired of newspaper and television reporters tagging every lame-brain thug with the name of my ancestors.

According to Webster's Dictionary, the term "hooligan" is from the Irish gangster Patrick Hooligan, who flourished around 1898 in Southwark, London. Now, I'm sure my great-great-great-uncle Paddy Hooligan paid his debt to society and never dreamed his ancestors would still be cringing 92 years later when the media reports on "hooligans arrested and taken away in a Paddy wagon"! Royko's recent remarks are prime examples of the anti-Hooligan sentiment that perniciously pervades the media today.

The consul general of Ireland here in Chicago, Gary Ansbro, tells me that "Hooligan, Houlihan, Holland, O'Hollihan and many other Irish names are all descendants of the original Gaelic name O'Hallachain. When political debate was outlawed in Ireland, many of her great writers would veil their nationalism by writing love poems to Kathleen ni Houlihan in the press. And John Holland, who lived in Ireland from 1841-1914, invented the submarine."

Mr. Ansbro also pointed out that the word "Tory," as in Margaret Thatcher's Tory Party in England, comes from an original Gaelic word that meant vagabond or highwayman. While that seems appropriate to me, I can envision a day centuries from now when the mayor, sheriff and other assorted Cook County politicians are all ruling members of the Hooligan Party.

As I have catalogued these slights to the Hooligan family name over the years, the one that most indelibly sticks in my memory is from the late '60s. The Berlin Wall was still a terrifying fact of life in Germany, and three men dropped their pants and mooned the East German guards. They were arrested and charged with "malicious hooliganism." I was never prouder.

So lay off the Hooligans. Their long history as freedom fighters, inventors and patriots more than makes up for the mistakes of Paddy Hooligan in 1898. And long live the Hooligan Party!

Mike Houlihan

INTRODUCTION

Hi everybody, it's your old friend Mike Houlihan here. Thanks for picking up my book.

Keep this book in your bathroom because it's the perfect companion piece while sitting on the throne.

I've tried to include what I consider my best stuff over the last 15 years.

These columns are arranged in chronological order. I had initially intended to categorize them according to subject, but then I realized that the subject matter shifted from show biz, politics, pals, faith, to stuff that couldn't really be labeled at all. So I figured let the columns come at the reader the way they were written, one at a time and all over the map.

I'm not sure but I'd also like to think that I became a better writer over the years so the stuff in the back of the book technically should be the best. So feel free to read it backwards if you are so inclined.

My thanks to my lovely wife Mary and my terrific sons Bill and Paddy for letting me bounce the stories off them before I filed them. Mary and the boys would take turns reading this stuff out loud and they really helped me decide if I thought something was funny or not.

Also big thanks to my old pal, the late Denis Gosselin, editor of the Chicago Tribune Sunday magazine. He gave me my first paid gig as a writer and got me started on this nonsense with his encouragement.

Michael Cooke, Editor in Chief of the Chicago Sun-Times, let me play with my column "Houli in 'da Hood" for three years and helped me develop a brand. Thanks Cookie.

Most of all I'd like to thank Irish American News editor and publisher, Cliff Carlson, who gave me the gig of Hooliganism, and never, ever, censored anything I have written. I guess his hands-off approach is pretty obvious in some of my columns but most editors wouldn't have the guts to trust a writer and Cliff did. Thanks pal.

Also thanks to you, the reader. People sometimes stop me on the street and will tell me they are loyal readers of Hooliganism and that makes me very happy. So keep it up!

Thanks again, and I hope you find this book entertaining.

Mike Houlihan

CHAPTER ONE

1993-1997

DON'T TOUCH MY FRIES, MA!

Chicago Tribune Sunday Magazine
September 19, 1993

As I walked into the audition room and picked up the script for the commercial, I noticed that the character I would be reading for was described as "a sorry looking man". Great, I thought, now I know what type the talent agency thinks I am.

Going on commercial auditions as an actor was all part of my "comeback" plan developed after an absence from show business of about ten years. Well, an absence from acting in show business anyway. I had continued to produce shows over the years and found it be more lucrative than thesping. But I still yearned for that old thrill of trodding the boards, the adulation of the audience, the laughter, the tears, the pained expressions. Besides, if I could earn five grand in one year, I got free health insurance through the union!

So here I was auditioning for a Burger King spot as the "sorry looking man." The part called for an actor who is dominated by his mother and has memory lapses because of the incredible stress she places on him. The character would have to be developed through the Stanislavski method so that I could actually feel his angst when he couldn't remember that saying "I love this Place" garnered you a discount on your cheeseburger. He also should look big and dumb. I got the part.

We shot the commercial at a Burger King in Naperville a few days later. The great thing about being a working actor is that they treat you like a star, when you're working. When you're trying to get work however, you are usually treated like a platypus with a highly contagious disease. As you're hopping up and down at auditions and barking like a dog or singing an insipid jingle you start to wonder if the "comeback" is worth it. But then you arrive on location and have make-up, wardrobe, and production assistants cooing over you and it all makes sense.

There is a never ending supply of tasty treats and fine cuisine on location and the toughest decision you'll ever have to make is whether you're having cold pop, hot chocolate, coffee, tea, or Evian water. The food is provided by something called "Craft Service" and is usually staffed by a stunningly attractive young lady with a name like Kiki. As I sidled up to the Craft Service table to inquire of Kiki, who was sunbathing on the hood of a car on the set, if she would be providing a hot meal for lunch, she burst my bubble by replying, "I think they are looking for you inside." and leveling me with a stare that said, "Don't forget you're playing the fat guy!"

My partner in the commercial was a very talented and seasoned actress named Caitlin Hart, AKA "Cat", who played my mother. Cat and I and the director, Rob, worked through the lines of the script shooting at the Burger King counter and tables with a crew of about twenty gaffers, productions assistants, technicians, cameramen, and assorted geniuses. I knew my classical training and years of performing Shakespeare were paying off when the crew laughed at my stupid expressions and goofy grin.

It was a great day of working with real pros and everybody genuinely felt we had the makings of a boffo commercial, especially when Rob suggested that my character, SAMMY, throw in the line, "Don't touch my fries, Ma!" This became the tag line to the commercial and by now I was dreaming that DON'T TOUCH MY FRIES, MA!" could do for me what "Where's the beef?" did for Clara Peller.

Nothing happened for about a month. Of course I got my check and paid a couple of bar tabs, but no calls from the coast. I had almost forgotten about my "comeback" when I was snoozing one Sunday afternoon on the couch and one of my kids shouted from the TV room, "Dad, your commercial!"

I leapt from my siesta to catch the last line, DON'T TOUCH MY FRIES, MA! Hey, that's me! "Pretty funny, Dad." The ultimate judges had deigned it acceptable and I was humbled by their gracious approval. I plopped myself down in front of the tube, "Get outta my chair." unleashed the fury of my samurai thumb on the remote control and was rewarded with a wash of ego gratification as it played about ten times over the next four hours. My wife even got excited, "Do you get paid every time it's on?" Sorry, honey, no.

Over the next ten days the commercial played relentlessly. Friends and relatives called for "Sammy" and guys in the street shouted, "Hey, the Burger King dude! Don't touch my fries, ma!" My friends at the bank called and ribbed me, "We gave that guy a mortgage?" While out on the South Side for a wake I stopped into one of my old haunts and was treated like a celebrity. Chanting, SAM-MY, SAM-MY, Jimmy MacKinnon actually bought me a drink. I was in heaven!

But "pride goeth before the fall."

Exactly twelve days after my debut as I was just finishing up at the office around five, (getting ready to call my driver Reginald to bring the limo around), I got a call from my old friend Joe Howard. "Your fifteen minutes of fame is up. The Channel Five news just did a story on your commercial. A group of retarded citizens objected to your characterization. Burger King has pulled the ad. You looked too much like a moron!"

I couldn't believe it. I called Channel Five and they confirmed that they had done a story that night on the Burger King commercial. The next day I got a tape of the broadcast.

Carol Marin had led the story with her usual smug serious expression,"A controversy tonight over the Burger King chain, blah, blah, blah... in the commercial a middle aged man portrays...." Whoa, middle aged? me? Well, ok maybe I am, but then I do believe that you, Carol, are also "of a certain age."

The news story featured an interview with a woman who has a child suffering from Down's Syndrome and she claimed that the commercial had just destroyed all the work she had done to convince her child she was normal. Huh? The Chicago Association of Retarded Citizens (CARC) put a spokeswoman on the air who said the commercial promoted "societal ignorance."

The reporter on the story, Sylvia Gomez, reassured viewers that the "individual in the commercial is not disabled or retarded, he's just an actor".

Burger King issued a statement that it was meant to be funny, that they were pulling the commercial off the air, and that the whole thing was a misunderstanding." I'll say!

I sat in stunned silence as I played the commercial over and over. There had never been any discussion of portraying Sammy as retarded or disabled. Stupid, yes. Oh, excuse me, "intellectually challenged". What we in Chicago commonly refer to as a "mope", hopefully a lovable mope. As a matter of fact the character was created in the great tradition of Frankie Fontaine, Crazy Guggenheim, Gomer Pyle, and Shakespeare's many clowns and fools. And these politically correct storm troopers had just killed him. It was the most embarrassing moment in my career since doing a show at Goodman Theatre in '73, when my pants split up the seam and 800 people began laughing at my family jewels.

It's all over now. I can't blame Burger King, they're in the business of making people happy and there's no point in angering any support groups. Friends I spoke with who have children with Down's Syndrome said they took no offense. The videotape of the commercial and news story make for lots of laughs at parties. For awhile I plotted starting a group called Overweight Middle-Aged Guys, (OWMAG) to get George Wendt, John Candy, Chris Farley, and their ilk kicked off the air. "Hey, they're makin' fun of me!"

Two weeks later I get a call from a talent agent asking me to audition for a McDonald's commercial.

"Since the Burger King spot is off the air, you can do this without a conflict, right?"

"Yes, yes, I can."

"You'll be reading for the part of Frankenstein."

Great. Unfortunately I will be out of town that day. But I would've done it. I mean, after all, I gotta keep that health insurance going, don't I? The comeback continues....

GROWING UP IRISH

Chicago Tribune Sunday Magazine
March 19, 1995

When I was a kid, every Irish mother wished and hoped and prayed that one of her sons would become a priest. And many of them did. The seminaries in those days were filled with Irish boys whose mom had steered them to the life of the cloth. But most of us eventually succumbed to some form of temptation and went on to other careers. That's also why there were so many Irish cops and politicians. It's sort of like being a priest, but you could still have sex. Let me tell you what happened to me.

I arrived on the Southside of Chicago sometime in 1950 when I was about two years old. We had moved from a two flat my Dad owned in West Rogers Park and I don't remember anything of my first two years, so I guess you could say my life <u>began</u> on the Southside of Chicago at 94th and Hamilton.

I was the youngest of seven kids, 5 older brothers and one older sister, and my existence fluctuated from being spoiled rotten as the baby or being completely ignored. My Mom would always introduce me as "the baby of the family, the last of the Mohicans!" I didn't know at the time how she knew I would be the last, but you could pretty much tell from my Dad's grumpy expression, that she had been practicing that old form of Irish birth control known as, "Nix on the nookey!"

Our neighborhood was known as CK, Christ the King Parish, and my first exposure to what "Power" was all about.

The power in our neighborhood was equally divided between the 19th Ward Democratic Organization and the parish. The Absolute power in the ward was the Alderman, Tommy Fitzpatrick, an old buddy of my Dad's. I got my first taste of political power when I was about ten years old one Halloween when the Beverly Theatre was holding a "spook-a-thon" of assorted cartoons for kids that day with Casper cartoons, prizes, costumes, giveaways, etc. They told me to hang on to my ticket stub to see if I won a prize.

As I was entering the lobby of the theatre, I ran into Mike Fitzpatrick, Alderman Tommy's son, and he handed me another ticket stub.

Mike Fitz strode up to me with a big smile on his face and said, "Throw that other stub away and use this one."

"Why Fitz? What's wrong with this one?"

Fitz looked at me in disbelief, "It ain't a winner, use this one."

When my number was called and they gave me a brand new baseball bat and glove for my prize I began to understand the awesome power of the 19th Ward Regular Democratic Organization.

The church emanated power, it was a beautiful new church built in 1953 and every Sunday, everybody was there for Mass. The most powerful person in CK was of course the Monsignor Patrick J. Gleason, our pastor. Monsignor was an "old world" type of pastor that you don't see much of anymore. He wore the purple socks, he drove a Cadillac that the parishioners had bought him and he used to drop in at our house unannounced.

The doorbell would ring and I would answer it and there would be the monsignor at the front door. "Hey Dad, Monsignor Gleason's here!" My dad would jump up from his chair, rebuttoning his pants, "Hiya Pat, come on down the basement." They'd go down to the basement bar and have a few pops and an hour later Monsignor would leave with money in his pocket and a load on. This is when I started to think that maybe it wouldn't be such a bad idea to become a priest.

My two oldest brothers had left the seminary by this time. Paul finished high school at St.Rita, but my brother Danny went the longest and I'm sure all those years of solitude and subterfuge in the seminary prepared him for his career in politics, in the 19th Ward! He left the seminary and went on to law school and was my mom's golden boy. But mom still wanted a priest in the family and with my brothers Willie, John and Tommy practically poster boys for reform school, I became the most likely candidate.

My mom was known as the holiest lady in the parish. She said the rosary about twenty times a day, and we had religious pictures all over our house. She even had an eight foot statue of the Blessed Mother erected in our backyard, and every year we would have a May Crowning of the statue. My sister was designated as "May Queen" and would crown the statue. There wasn't a vote.

One of the other statues was a smaller one in our living room of St. Michael the Archangel. He had long blond flowing hair, but looked real macho with his armor on over his wings, and a big silver sword in his right hand. Under his left foot, being crushed, was some sort of weird looking four legged monster with a pissed off look on his face, obviously Lucifer. My brothers used to stick cigarette butts out in Lucifer's mouth and leave them for my mom to find later.

Even though I was only about nine years old, my mom started a full-blown campaign to get me to join the priesthood and enroll in the seminary upon graduation from eighth grade. My brothers had both been in the seminary for The Columban Fathers, a group of missionaries who spread the word of God to third world countries, most of them with an Irish brogue. We had priests over at our house constantly anyway, so when my Mom informed them that I was going to be a priest too, I was invited to sit and listen to them while they drank my old man's booze and told stories of the Philippines, China, and Malaysia, and I really got into it.

I used to imagine that I would be sort of a Bing Crosby type priest and would be able to flirt with nuns like Ingrid Bergman.

Of course my brothers weren't buying it. "You little suck-up, you ain't gonna be no priest." I was sharing a bedroom with my brother Tommy in those days and as we talked at night before falling asleep he would spin tales of girls brassieres and girdles as he tried to question my commitment to the priesthood. He would always start with "So, ya wanna be a priest, huh? Did I tell ya I saw the outline of Fran Pistelli's nipple while she was playing volleyball the other day? Whaddya think of that, Father Mike?"

I was probably not old enough then to fathom the implications of the vision of the outline of Fran Pistelli's nipple, but that image stayed with me even as the Columban Fathers continued to recruit me. They brought me to White Sox games, out for burgers, my mom used to send me over to the Columban House at 88th and Hamilton to serve mass for these guys at six o'clock in the morning! And I liked it! I would hang around the Columban House, it was a huge mansion with a private chapel, and drink Hires Root Beer in their kitchen while the ladies from the old country prepared corned beef and cabbage for lunch and listened to the "Irish Hour' on the radio.

My "holy act" put me in great stead with my mom and all the nuns at school when I would announce that "I'm going to be a priest!" I would fantasize about being a missionary in China and being tortured by the commies because I wouldn't renounce Jesus, and if I was lucky they would execute me and I would of course go straight to heaven. But what I really wanted to be was a powerful guy like Monsignor Gleason, wearing the purple socks, driving a Cadillac, flirting with the good looking nuns, hanging out at parishioners homes drinking their booze and everybody sort of looking up to me and fearing me at the same time.

But if the thought of commie chinks torturing me couldn't question my vocation, then there was something just as powerful that could. I was in seventh grade one Sunday afternoon and shooting baskets in my backyard with Bill McFarland. When the ball rolled into the garage, McFarland ran in there to retrieve it.

"Hey Houli, come here."

As he was getting the ball in the garage he had spied three Playboy magazines laying on the backseat of my brother's Volkswagen. We looked around and got in the car and started perusing. I opened to a photograph of a young lady named Krista Speck, (no relation to Richard), and her abundant charms were like a blinding light that knocked me off my priest pedestal, sort of the reverse of what happened to Saul of Tarsus when he became the apostle Paul.

My blood began to boil and I started to feel like I was going to explode. After ten minutes of frying our brains on the Playboys we didn't feel much like shootin' baskets anymore. McFarland got this real itchy look and said, " I better be goin' home now." Yeah sure, get the hell out of here so I can sneak these Playboys up to my room for a more in depth examination.

I resigned myself to the fact that I wasn't priest material after all. There just weren't that many nuns who looked as good as Krista Speck. And at the age of twelve, she was a lot more enticing than the thought of being a missionary and having Chinese communists ramming bamboo shafts under my toenails.

So I didn't become a priest, I became an actor. Sorry mom, but the chances of meeting Krista Speck were better in show business than in the monastery.

ST. PATRICK'S DAYS

Irish American News
March 1996

About ten years ago, I was taking a bus home down Second Avenue in New York City on St. Patrick's Day. It was about midnight and as I glanced out the window, I caught sight of two muscular bouncers tossing an inebriated little fella out of one of the many Irish bars that populate the street. They were laughing as they watched him stumble to his feet and adjust the souvenir derby he'd been wearing all day. And when he cursed them and started to disgorge the very large volume of green beer he'd consumed that night into his derby, they laughed even harder. He staggered before them, staring into his beloved derby, now filled to the brim with his holiday cheer. Then his wizened face crinkled and he turned on the two lads with a twinkle in his eye. Their laughter turned to shock as the leprechaun pitched his hatful of spew all over both of them and their snappy green sweaters as well as the entire front window of Delaney's and he scampered down the street.

I've always liked St. Patrick's Day. Sure it's a great day for all Irish and Irish-Americans to celebrate our ancestry with parades, rebel songs, dancing, and toasts. Lots of toasts. But for me it always conjures up memories of St. Patrick's Days of my past and the hope that another Irish adventure could be marching it's way into my heart. It's a day filled with romance, music, bravado, laughter and very seldom tears. It's day that has left many an indelible image etched upon my soul.

My earliest memories of St. Patrick's Day were as a kid growing up on the southwest side of Chicago. I guess I was about five when my Dad came home one day and announced that "he" had been invited to march in the parade that year. This was an honor for our whole family and all seven kids were bundled and trundled downtown that day to see my Dad. We cheered as he strode smiling up the street with Alderman Tommy Fitzpatrick and the 19th Ward at his side as the Shannon Rovers piped "The Minstrel Boy". The fact that there were about five thousand other ruddy-faced Irish guys also being honored as they stomped along didn't matter. We loved it.

♣

As teenagers growing up on the Southside in the sixties, we didn't have heavy metal music or MTV. We did have the Clancy Brothers, however. The Clancy Brothers, (Tommy, Paddy, Liam, and Tommy Makem), were Irish folk singers who were barnstorming across America, riding the crest of the folk singer craze, and stirring the chords of Irish-American pride which by now has become an industry. We had all their albums and they were played continuously around St. Patrick's Day in every house with an Irish moniker. We'd tramp around the neighborhood singing "The Wild Colonial Boy" and guys who knew all the words to "Johnny McEldoo", a speedy tongue twister that was sung in jig time, were regarded with high esteem. It was music the whole family could enjoy and sing along with. It could also drive you nuts listening to the "diddley diddley dee" for hours on end. Our "Clancy Brothers Greatest Hits" album was destroyed one night when it was flung across the living room and shattered on the wall by my brother Bill who could not stand another minute of my brother Johnny's interpretation of "Jug of Punch".

I was working for the Sanitary District as a janitor in my early twenties when my boss Jack Sullivan noticed my bright green iridescent pants and grandly announced, "It's St. Patrick's Day, why don't you take the rest of the day off and go to the parade." I was gone before he could reconsider and spent the rest of the afternoon frolicking with my Irish brethren. I wound up asleep at home by dinnertime. The front door bell awakened me and my Dad informed me that, "Joe Kivlehan's at the door for ya!" Joe was a nodding acquaintance and I wondered why he would be stopping by to see me this fine day. Perhaps he had heard about my green pants and wanted to see them for himself! As I stepped out onto the front porch, Joe wished me "Happy St. Patrick's Day fathead!" and then punched me in the nose, "and that's for what you said to my sister at the parade!"

While living in New York, I produced a show Off-Broadway, A COUPLE OF BLAGUARDS, starring the McCourt Brothers from Limerick Ireland. St. Patrick's Day was our biggest night and we all went out to celebrate at Eamon Doran's Irish Pub. Ireland's Bunratty Castle Singers were also in town that night and had come to the show, in costume. I was enjoying a Guinness with our bodhrain player, Morris Kehoe, a lad from the old country, as we basked in the glory of our night, tapping our feet to the rhythm of the music, and drank in the beauty of the Bunratty Castle Singers. They were gorgeous Irish girls with flaming red hair and the bodice of their gowns were a deep Emerald green revealing cleavage like the hills of Ballybeg. Morris was staring into the eyes of one buxom lass with jet-black hair and skin like alabaster as he drooled into his stout. He was mumbling incoherently to himself and then he leaned over and whispered something into her ear. The music had reached a fever pitch just as she turned and looked him in the eye and a playful seductive smile played across her comely Irish features. It was cinematic! For one fleeting moment his words had become a magical aphrodisiac to her and the crimson blush of her cheek and breast said, "Tell me more!" What had he said? I had to know. Was it some romantic Gaelic phrase he had learned from the little people? "Morris, what did you just say to her?" He looked at me with a mischievous grin, and then stopped, looked bewildered, and then crestfallen as he whimpered to me in frustration, "I can't remember!"

♣

In the late '80's I was special events consultant to the State of Illinois Center, (now the James R. Thompson Building), producing ethnic celebrations throughout the year. "Illinois Salutes The Irish" was my favorite event and annually featured a raffled off trip to the old country, dignitaries from Ireland, traditional Irish music, the world champion Trinity Academy of Irish Dancing, the Emerald Society bagpipe band, and the piece de resistance: Alderman Eddie Burke playing the piano and former Senate President Phil Rock warbling "Galway Bay", and their encore number, "Danny Boy".

We packed the auditorium every year for the St. Patrick's Day show and one year were lucky enough to have the Taoiseach himself. (the Prime Minister of Ireland), making an appearance and wishing the people of Illinois a Happy St. Patrick's Day.

We only had one dressing room and so I had all the dignitaries assemble there before the show. There I was standing in a room no larger than my kitchen with Governor Thompson, Eddie Burke, Phil Rock, The Consul General of Ireland, and the Taoiseach! So I start shooting the breeze with these magnificos, feeling like the proverbial fly on the wall when I felt the pincers of a hand nip the shoulder of my suit and draw me out of the room. It was Elizabeth, the Governor's officious, hyperactive advance person, and her disdain for me was palpable as she yanked me out of the inner sanctum and into the hallway. "There's no need for you to be in there now."

I had suddenly been transported back in time to grammar school and the visage of this bureaucratic witch morphed into my seventh grade nun, Sister Philothea. "That's too bad," I said as I headed down the stairs to the stage, "cause we were all just about to get naked!"

"Don't think you're going to get away with that remark!" she screeched at me from the top of the stairs. "Of course I'll get away with it, it's St. Patrick's Day."

♣

"Getting away with it." has become my coda for the measure of a truly great St. Patrick's Day. And the greatest St. Patrick's Day of my life occurred when I was eighteen and a senior in high school.

Like most Irish Catholic boys, my mother had always wanted me to be a priest. I had toyed with this idea until puberty when more practical concerns steered me towards considering a career as a movie star. But if I wasn't going to be priest...who said I couldn't dress up like a priest. I still had that yearning for a vocation.

And so I found a black sport coat, cut the top half off an altar boy cassock I had "borrowed" from the sacristy of my church, tucked it into my black pants, and wore a white shirt backwards under the cassock. It was a crude costume, but it looked convincing. Would it be convincing to teenage girls I wondered? The only way to find out was to test it out.

The plan was to drop into Mother McCauley Girls High School at around two in the afternoon on St. Patrick's Day and attempt to pass as a priest. My friend Jack Whalen and I were especially hoping to encounter some girls with "Kiss Me I'm Irish" buttons on their lapels. We walked in and announced to the lady at the door that we were Fathers Kelly and McGillicuddy from the Propagation of the Faith and wanted to thank the girls for their mission collections. She told us she would have to check with the principal.

This sent a chill through my bones. What if the principal was a nun and didn't buy our disguises? What if she asked me some ecclesiastical questions to trip me up? We retreated down the hall and were immediately enveloped in a sea of 500 teenage girls as the bell rang releasing the students for the day.

Jack and I went into our best renditions of charming Irish priests as we talked to the girls with our phony brogues. "Ah sure and your a beautiful colleen, wudja like to confess yer sins to Father Kelly?" The colleens in question seemed nonplussed by our piety as they scrambled to get home that Friday. We're lucky we weren't killed in the stampede of girls exiting school for the weekend. We were picked up in the current and spewed out the doors with the rest of them. But just as we passed the main entrance, a man waiting to pick up his daughter from school, tipped his hat to us. We had gotten away with it!

CHRISTMAS IN THE BASEMENT

WBEZ Public Radio
December 1996

When I was a kid, my sister Mary would give me a lovely gift every year for Christmas. Usually something expensive like a ballpoint pen. I was not the only recipient of her largesse; my five brothers would also each receive one of the wonderfully wrapped pens. Mary would hand you the cylindrical package with this look of endearment as she solemnly intoned, "Merry Christmas, Mike", as if she were surrendering the Hope diamond. And I'd stare at this tiny stick of rolled wrapping paper and turn to my brothers and say, "Gee, I wonder what this could be?"

But it still wasn't bad compared to my brother Johnny's annual gift of wallet-sized photos of himself with the inscription, "Love, John."

It wasn't that they were cheap; it's just that with seven kids in our family you had to spread your five-buck present allotment money around. Of course all us kids would make sure we got Mom a really nice present like a rosary. My Dad was harder to shop for since he had no hobbies other than bringing his pals down to the bar in our basement. I once bought him a pretzel holder with a porcelain figure of a bartender who looked like Mister Dunahey, the guy on the Jackie Gleason show. He liked that alot.

Our basement was the place where the Christmas spirit held sway all through November and December. On Christmas morning us kids would all run downstairs where the tree was set up and tear the place apart looking for Santa's loot. During the holidays the basement bar was decorated with little green and red lights and my Dad would serve Labatt's to his friends because he liked the green bottles.

I fell off a bar stool during one of our holiday parties when I was around nine and had to get stitches. My Dad and his pal Tommy Fitzpatrick had me back from the hospital just in time to hang our stockings. I remember Mister Fitzpatrick saying, "It won't be the last bar stool he battles!" I didn't get it then, but of course he was right.

The atmosphere of the basement was sacred because of all the great presents that had been unveiled there each Christmas over the years. Running downstairs to discover a train set chugging around the tree, or hearing my Dad swear a blue streak as he tried to assemble my first Schwinn, had imbued the room with an aura that spoke to us kids and said, "Forget the sugarplums, this is where the toys will be!"

The coolest Christmas of all was the year we got the jukebox. It was a 1956 Wurlitzer with glowing lights and bubbles packed with tunes by the Mills Brothers, Rosemary Clooney, and Tennessee Ernie Ford singing "Sixteen Tons". This was a gift for the whole family and as we came downstairs on Christmas eve for the presentation Bing Crosby was warbling "White Christmas" and my Dad was behind the bar, beaming.

I ran to the Wurlitzer and pressed my face up against the glass searching for my favorite tune. And there it was. "The Chipmunk Song", Alvin and the Chipmunks singing, "I Still Want A Hula-Hoop". And it was free, free! He had the machine rigged up so that no coins were required for your ecstasy.

"B-Seven" became my mantra. I'd hit the buttons and watch as a sickle shaped arm popped up and descended into the rack of black '45's and returned with B7 firmly in its' grasp, pivoting perpendicularly to the left, and delivering the Chipmunk song to the turntable. Plunking a barstool down in front of the juke-box, I glued myself to the pane as the green and red lights from the bubbles played off my face, and I'd watch the needle drop on B-7, blasting out the melody of the Chipmunks all the way into January.

The grooves in record B-7 began to wear and the needle would stick. The most annoying refrains of that classic tune would play over and over and over. "Alvin...Alvin...ALVIN!" Until one of my brothers would kick the box. That was the only way they could stop it because I would shield the reject button with my wiry body and refuse to give up the song. I simply couldn't understand why anyone would prefer der Bingle to Alvin.

And then one night it was gone. I came downstairs and hit B7 and the arm descended into the black pile and came up empty. B7 no longer existed. My brother Johnny pointed to an ashtray on the bar piled high with triangular chunks of black vinyl. "Is this what you're lookin' for?" he said with a chuckle.

I felt betrayed by my own family. Who had done such a dastardly thing? What venal soul had destroyed my beloved Chipmunk song? Who did this? Johnny shook his head and delivered the sad news that every kid encounters sooner or later. "Sorry Mike, Santa Claus was sick of it."

THE 94TH STREET CHRISTMAS CAROLERS

Irish American News
December 1996

Mrs. Fleming stood in her doorway with arms folded as we all sang "The First Noel" as loudly as possible. She didn't seem impressed with our talents as we finished and sort of milled around kicking the snow off our boots, coughing, standing on her porch and hoping she would give us some dough. But when Kathy Brucks suggested we start up again with "Oh Little Town of Bethlehem", Mrs. Fleming sprung into action.

"Oh that was wonderful children, here's a dollar, why don't you take your caroling next door now to Mrs. Finns'." as she shoved the money into Kathy's hands, slammed the front door, and turned the light out on her porch. We knew it wasn't the singing that was earning us money. It was stopping the singing that got us the biggest tips.

The idea of going Christmas caroling had at first seemed wimpy to me and my eleven-year-old pals. Didn't we do enough of that junk at mass with the nuns breathin' down our necks? But the money angle hadn't occurred to me until we saw the girls on our block leaving Mrs. Herman's house with hot cocoa on their breath and quarters in their mittens. Donny Finn, Jimmy Grogarty, and me were poised with snowballs to cream the girls as they left the old lady's porch when we heard her say, "Now, did everybody get a quarter?"

Suddenly I had visions of us joining the Vienna Boys Choir, but I rejected the idea when Grogarty told me that most of those guys had been castrated to keep their voices high. But what about the 94th Street Boys Choir? All we'd have to do was get a book of Christmas carols and start hitting every house on our block. We'd put everybody in the holiday mood. It'd be like trick or treatin' for money!

We started rehearsing in my basement until my mom kicked us out of the house. After listening to "Walking In A Winter Wonderland" for the twentieth time, she said we needed more than just our gang to do the caroling. Our voices were just starting to change that year and there was just too much creaking and croaking. Sort of like alley cats with puberty problems.

There was nothing to do but team up with the girls to form a more appealing group of Christmas carolers and to insure higher tips for our celestial singing. Surprisingly, the girls on our block were all for this idea. They didn't seem to care that much about the money although they weren't about to give up their share of the loot. But they seemed to genuinely get a kick out of all us walking together through the snow and assembling on some poor sucker's porch as we launched into our sure fire rendition of "Hark The Heralds Angels Sing". Kathy Brucks sort of took over as choir director and made the reasonable suggestion that us boys just hum through most of the songs.

We started at the first house on the corner of 94th and Hamilton and worked our way up to 95th Street. We'd just start singing and ringing the doorbell at the same time just in case they didn't hear us.

There was always an awkward moment after the first song was finished and we'd look at the people waiting for them to either request another song or make the obligatory drop. Most of them got the message pretty quick when Fat Jackie Whalen would waddle toward the front of our group and launch into his worst rendition of "Oh Holy Night".

But a funny thing happened on one of our final missions as carolers of 94th street. It was right before Christmas and we had done pretty well that night, maybe a buck and a half a piece so far. We had one more house to hit and it was old Mrs. Mix, who was a widow and lived alone in her gray bungalow with the yard full of weeds. There were no lights on in her house and the walk hadn't been shoveled but we thought we'd take a crack at her anyway. We went through "Jingle Bells", "Little Drummer Boy", and even "Adeste Fidelis" but still no sign of ol' Mrs. Mix.

Fat Jackie got mad and started bangin' on the door. "Come on, we know you're in there!" The girls restrained him as we started down the steps to leave. And then Fat Jackie turned and stood on her bottom step and delivered his cruelest curse to those who didn't pay. The Fat Jackie Whalen solo version of "Silent Night."

The light from the moon illuminated his breath as he stood there defiantly. And suddenly it didn't sound half bad. It actually started to sound pretty good, beautiful even, as if God wouldn't let Jackie hurt poor ol' Mrs. Mix. As we watched from the walk I spied a figure in the upstairs window peeking down at Jackie. Maybe it was just the night or maybe the cold and the moonlight and the vapor of our breath but I could swear I saw her smiling as Jackie, who sounded like Mario Lanza at this point, hit the high note of "sleep in heavenly peace." As he finished we heard someone shout, "Merry Christmas" and all us kids, Jackie included, shouted it back "Merry Christmas!"

EULOGY FOR AN IRISH TAVERN

Chicago Tribune Sunday Magazine
March 16, 1997

"Hey Houli, who died?" This was the greeting I received from Jimmy Goff every time I entered the New Evergreen bar at 91st and Western for the last ten years. It seemed like every opportunity I had to visit Southside Irish haunts was after attending a wake for old pals and relatives. As you get older you spend more time hitting the wake circuit. I had even come close one night to scoring a "triple double" by mingling at three wakes all in one funeral parlor. Hence Jimmy's plaintive cry across the bar every time I walked in the door, "Hey Houli, who died?"

The New Evergreen bar burned to the ground on Friday morning May 24th. I never thought I'd be mourning the death of a tavern, but this was no ordinary gin mill.

It started as a roadhouse known as the Evergreen Gardens around 1912 when Western Ave was just a one-lane dirt road. You could meet some nice girls there in the twenties and thirties when the back room doubled as a dime-a-dance joint. Some bad guys almost bumped off Machine Gun Jack McGurn one night at the Wisconsin-Central tracks on 91st street as he was leaving the Evergreen. They added an 18-hole golf course behind the bar around 1921 and dubbed it the "Evergreen Park Country Club", not for members only. Babe Ahern's family had owned the property since the turn of the century and she had watched dozens of different bar owners work the site until Skip Carey showed up in November of 1984.

Skip and I had done time together at Christ the King grammar school in the late fifties and sixties. Punky McFarland had coined his nickname in fifth grade when she came into class one morning after watching the TV show "You Asked For It" sponsored by Skippy peanut butter. "You look just like the kid in the ad!" From that day on it stuck. Lots of folks never knew Skip Carey's real name. Skip was a Chicago cop before getting into the bar business.

Saturday night was Karioke night at the New Evergreen. The first Tuesday of every month you could "Stop in For a Psychic Reading", as the sign on their marquee, said. Skip called those Tuesdays "Psycho Night".

"We had live entertainment in there for the first six years. There was a band on Friday nights called the Playboys, they were great, two used car salesmen. One guy's name was Murph, had this wild toupee and he'd take his shoes off while he played the drums, cracking corny jokes, trying to pick up girls. They were horrible."

But the main source of entertainment was the bar. It was a beautiful mahogany built in the thirties in the shape of an oval. There were 35 bar stools and wherever you looked there was action. "I could have enemies in there and as long as they were at opposite ends of the bar it was okay, they could stand and stare at each other."

Over the years Skip threw hundreds of benefits in the back room for policeman, fireman, political fundraisers, and many of the more significant events of Southsider's lives. Bachelor parties were big, but so were christenings. "Lots of people got married in that back room, not many of them lasted. I used to call it the wayward chapel."

Every St. Patrick's Day the New Evergreen was the first stop for foolish souls attempting the infamous "deathwalk". The "deathwalk" was a legendary Southside Irish tradition of hitting every bar on Western Avenue from 91st street to 119th Street and the customary starting shot was always hoisted at the New Evergreen.

On the morning of the fire Skip got a call at home that his tavern was burning. He got over there in time to hear the fireman say, "It's such a blaze, we're not gonna go in, we'll control it and let it burn out." He watched it go up in smoke.

Froggy McGuire was supposed to be throwing a birthday party in the back room that night for his girlfriend Mary Pat Moran. They moved it to the Beverly Woods, but after the fire it seemed more like a wake.

Skip said the death of the bar, "Left a void in the neighborhood, especially for people our age. There weren't a lot of kids in there, mostly thirty and up. Lots of oldtimers, the moms and dads of kids I grew up with."

When you own a bar there's a mystique to your personality, people come to you with everything, their tickets, getting a job, advice, almost like being an alderman. And you want to help them, steer them in the right direction. You lose that, you feel kind of lost. You almost lose your identity. Your identity is your bar and you carry that with you wherever you go.

It was just a neighborhood joint with a room in the back for parties.But they treated you right and made you feel at home.

So who died Jimmy? Another old pal died. And maybe a little piece of you and me and John "Skippy" Carey and the rest of the old gang who stopped into the New Evergreen on their way through life.

And that's the way it would have ended if it weren't for the pluck of the Irish. It won't be ready for St. Patrick's Day but Skip'll be opening his new place this Spring, just a few blocks from the old one. So spread the word to the old gang that they'll always be welcome at "Skip's New Evergreen" on 87th street, just west of Western. And tell those boyos on the Southside to start getting in shape because the "deathwalk" just got a lot longer.

NO FIGHTIN' ON ST. PATRICK'S DAY

Irish American News
March 1997

I sucker punched a bully in the Blarney Stone tavern on Eighth Avenue in New York City on St. Patrick's Day about twenty years ago. I was a lot younger then and he was so drunk he could barely stand up, especially after I smashed him right in the kisser. It felt great. Not for him of course, but I felt like John L. Sullivan as the patrons of the bar swarmed around me, buying me drinks, and congratulating me on my victory.

As they tossed him out into the street I felt almost sorry for the guy. He had obviously started his celebrating too early and was haranguing everybody in sight as he threw the booze down his huge gullet and banged on the bar. By the time my pals and me came in after the parade he was getting pretty ornery. He staggered over to our table and slapped me in the face for no reason. He was asking for it all right and I was happy to oblige as I jumped up on my chair, grabbed him by the throat to steady his swaying, and fired away. He looked really surprised as he backed away and I delivered a farewell kick to his family jewels.

I'd had my share of St. Patrick's Day scrapes as a young lad growing up in Chicago, but this was the first donnybrook I ever came out of unscathed. I can still remember that bleak day in March of '69 when two brothers from Limerick played football with my head one night in Hanley's House of Happiness. "Give 'em the shoes, Liam!" one boyo yelled as his brother boxed my ears with his brogans.

So I could sympathize with my new friend as they tossed his hat into the street after him. I knew what his tomorrow was going to be like. You awake with a new understanding of the intricacies of the celebration of our patron saint. And as you grope toward the faucet with the thirst of a salamander you catch sight of your bludgeoned face in the mirror. That's when a lot of guys decide they don't like St. Patrick's Day anymore and they swear it off completely. They spend years staying home that night watching the Duke and Victor McLaglen bash each other across the Inishfree countryside and wishing they could meet a girl like Maureen O'Hara.

But folks, it doesn't have to be that lonely. The most important thing to remember about the St. Patrick's Day celebration, especially now that it lasts the whole weekend, is that you must pace yourself. Take it easy and you will be able to last until the last call on Monday. Hey you can always rent THE QUIET MAN next weekend.

The weekend celebration can be great fun if you remember to pace yourself and control your emotions. It's much better to laugh than fight. Remember that you don't have to drink every beer in the joint and that the guy pinching your girlfriend at the bar is also probably a fellow Irishman and merely wants to show his appreciation of your excellent taste in women.

So get out there. Go to the parades, downtown and Southside. Visit Gaelic Park and the Irish American Heritage Center and your favorite Irish pub. Chow down on the corned beef and cabbage and quaff a few Guinness', but go easy. That's what we're supposed to be doing in celebration of our proud Irish heritage. No fightin', just singin', dancin', lovin', and laughin'. Happy St. Patrick's Day!

THE SIGN OF PEACE

Irish American News
WBEZ Public Radio
July 1997

The lady in the pew in front of me was praying devoutly when she suddenly sneezed into her hands. Uh-oh I thought to myself as I peered over her shoulder trying to determine if she was ill. My reasons were selfish, I confessed to myself as she let go with another sneezer right into her right palm. My worst fears were confirmed when I checked her hands for any sign of a handkerchief. Nope, she had kerchooed wetly into her naked hands.

Just then, Father Paul told the congregation to exchange a "sign of peace" with our neighbors. The little old lady turned to me with a beatific smile on her face that emanated love as she chirped, "May the peace of Our Lord be always with you." And then she thrust her disease ridden paw towards me.

My mind was racing as I contemplated the unthinkable. I flashed her my most sincere smile as I glanced down at her extended little peace offering. It looked so innocent. The hand that had washed a thousand dishes, raised and diapered her children and grandchildren, paid the paperboy and tousled his hair, and undoubtedly had caressed a million rosary beads was now imploring me to shake it in a simple act of faith. It didn't look wet. There were no visible signs of sneeze residue and yet I was sure a microscope would have exposed that hand as Typhoid Mary's twin.

I pictured myself grasping her hand in my best rendition of the old "shake the hand, that shook the hand, that shook the hand of John L. Sullivan" routine and delivering the best "sign of peace" she had ever experienced. But that little red devil with the horns and pitchfork was perched on my shoulder pouring venom into my ear. "Oh sure, she wants ya to share some of her delicious phlegm with ya! That's all ya need! Don't do it, you'll be sick for weeks, trying to shake that flu bug."

What's the protocol for this, I wondered. When the Cardinals and the Pope were designing this move at Vatican II back in the sixties, didn't anyone ask about contagion? Did this new dogma require the shaking of hands or just a simple verbal acknowledgement of Peace? And what about all that kissing that seems to suspiciously break out in abundance at every Christmas Eve midnight mass?

The new mass was radical enough when it went from Latin to English. We used to answer the priest's incantation of "Dominus Vobiscum" with what I always thought was God's telephone number, "Et cum spiri-2-2-0". Didn't any of those Cardinals suddenly ask, "Hey, what do we do if there's a little old lady in front of you who has just sneezed into her hands, twice?"

I looked into her eyes as she waited for me to return her greeting. For a moment they flickered as if to say, "Please don't break my heart." The little angel on my right shoulder shouted in my ear, "It's a leap of faith, go for it!" I was ready to offer my hand when the little red devil, who was starting to sound like Edward G. Robinson, jumped onto my left ear and said, "Sure, sure, a leap of faith, you're gonna leap yourself right into a hospital bed if you shake that hand, is that what ya want, yeah, yeah, is that what ya want wiseguy?"

Time had stopped. My smile was wilting. She started to look crestfallen as she gazed at my cowardly hand hiding now in my pocket. I could reach out and shake her by the wrist, what about that? Or maybe a little love pat punch on the shoulder, sort of a noogie for Peace.

"No, the hand, shake her hand, make the leap of faith."

"Are you nuts, give her the noogie, she's crawling with joims"

Suddenly she looked at me with pity, not anger, or scorn but sorrow at my unholy attitude. I was awash in a sea of shame and I blurted out "Peace Be With You" and really gave her my most personal, genuine "you", like we were old friends.

And then I raised my hands up and formed the time-out sign, left hand extended upwards and right hand perpendicular to the left. It was a sports signal, but it had a universal meaning and maybe she had seen the NBA playoffs and would interpret it as a confused explanation of my behavior. "Sorry, you see I can't make the leap of faith right now, but catch me next week when you're not sick and I won't disappoint you."

Edward G. Robinson was laughing his horns off on my left and my guardian angel whispered in my ear, "What a mope!"

Or was that the little old lady?

FRED THE DOG

Irish American News
WBEZ Public Radio
August 1997

We're in the midst of the dog days of summer and I recently found out that they are so-named because that is when astrologists say the Dog Star rises and sets with the sun. I have to assume they are referring to Pluto although I always thought Goofy was a bigger star, definitely a better actor. I'm sure there will be folks voting for Rin Tin Tin, Lassie, and Benjie, but as a great actor once put it, "Dying is easy, comedy is hard!" So Goofy goes down in my book as the number one Dog Star, followed closely behind by Farfel, the dog in the old Nestles commercials.

Psychologists say that a pet will often take on the character traits of the family members who care for it. I hope that's not true, because my dog Fred was a liar, thief, scoundrel, and lecher. That doesn't say much for me and my family I know, but I have to admit I was secretly proud of Fred's notorious reputation in our neighborhood.

He never did any tricks like sit, speak, beg; these were not in his repertoire. You could, however, always count on Fred to saunter into the center of the room when my Mom was having the ladies over from the Altar Guild Society and lie back on the rug and start licking himself. He loved being the center of attention, but it had to be on his terms.

Fred appeared to be just an ordinary beagle, but underneath that puppy dog look was the heart of a dissolute, debauched, old hound dog. He hated dog food, no matter how you prepared it. He'd watch us eat steak dinners and give us this look that said, "Oh thanks a lot, you're chowin' down on a Porterhouse and you expect me to eat that mush in my bowl. Come on, give it up.", and then he'd bark and whine and scratch your leg until you surrendered part of your supper. I once tried the same routine on him while he was eating, just to show him how annoying it was. I got down on all fours as he was dining at his bowl and barked, whined, and scratched his leg. And then he bit me.

My sister Mary and I were the supposed "owners" of Fred since he was given to us as a pup for her graduation and my Confirmation. This meant we were responsible for cleaning up the poops he would invariably leave on the kitchen floor since he refused to become housebroken. My mom's euphemism for this was a greeting card. She'd wake you up and tell you, "Freddy left a card for you this morning."

Fred never knew the meaning of "heel". He thought it was just another name my Dad would use to curse him out whenever he got off the leash. "Freddy you bum!" was Dad's mantra every time he walked out into our backyard. This was met by a frosty reception from our new next-door neighbor Fred Cunningham. Mister Cunningham didn't seem to like it any better when Dad switched to just screaming expletives which questioned Fred's parentage.

Every few weeks each summer Fred would escape off the leash and out of the backyard and go on a bender for a couple of days. Friends and neighbors would give us reports that he had been seen in the area cavorting with a group of bitches in heat, as if they were telling you tales of your drunken uncle. He'd always return like the prodigal son around midnight a few days later, covered in grime and smelling like fertilizer, as he pawed at the back door. I'd scold him as I gave him something to eat and wiped the dung off his ears and he'd look at me as if to say, "I know, I know, what can I tell ya, I'm a dog!"

The profligate life finally caught up with Fred when he was in his early seventies. Dog years. His stomach bloated up and he was also having trouble delivering his "cards". I drove him that last fateful mile to the vet's office as he sat shotgun. I looked at him sitting there in misery and tried to buck up his spirits, "Maybe it's not that bad Fred. Maybe the doc will give you some medicine to patch you up." He fixed me with a stoic gaze as if to say, "No kid, it's curtains. I know it and you know it. Just tell the croaker to make it quick and painless. I'll tell ya this though, I have no regrets. Not one. I just wanna go out with some class."

So tonight as I gaze up at the sky searching for that Dog Star in the heavens, I'm hoping for a glimpse of my old pal Fred. I miss his unique personality and unpretentious charm. I hope he's up there with Pluto, Goofy, and Farfel tonight, leaving his calling cards all over the Milky Way.

LET'S SEE YOUR UNION BUTTON

Irish American News
WBEZ Public Radio
September 1997

We didn't have any millionaires show up at the high school career day my alma mater sponsored for this year's senior class. There were plenty of lawyers, doctors, and accountants boasting about their professions, but the guys with the really big bucks were conspicuous by their absence. Somebody forgot to invite the plumbers, bricklayers, and electricians.

That's too bad because these days there aren't enough kids interested in a career in the trades. Everybody wants their kid to become a lawyer. Are they nuts? There are already too many lawyers slithering through society in the nineties. I can just imagine the chaos we have to look forward to with law schools spitting out more of their conniving graduates every year.

The future lawyers were all weaned on lousy TV shows about lawyers like Perry Mason, Matlock, Law & Order, ad nauseam. That's what started poisoning the young minds of America. They all wanted to be like those slick jerks on LA Law. Why don't we have any shows where the star is a plumber? Those mopes in Hollywood have no idea what goes on in the real world. And when they do feature a character on TV who is a tradesman they always portray him as practically penniless. But take a look at your bill next time you need one of these guys. They're pulling down much better bread than most lawyers and when their hands get dirty, they can wash 'em off.

The lack of young people joining the working class portends disaster for all of us. Nobody encourages American kids to become bricklayers or carpenters so you wind up with a few qualified craftsmen who can charge you an arm and a leg and the rest are guys right off the boat who pass themselves off as experts. Yanks are such suckers for any dolt with a foreign accent. The French chef in that downtown restaurant? Hey, he must be good because he can't speak English. He also can't read English and that means he's ignoring that sign in the mens room that says, "Employees Must Wash Hands"!

There won't be any red blooded American kids building schools, hospitals, or communities in the future. They'll all be in law school studying ways to sue the contractor who's gong to build their house. They should study hard too, because unless we start encouraging our kids to go into plumbing, masonry, or electrical work; those houses are going to be built by the Eastern European equivalent of the Three Stooges.

Somewhere along the line our kids have not considered the economic reality of their future. Kid gets out of high school and goes to college for four years running up student loans of close to a hundred grand. Then he hitches up for law school at another hundred grand. By the time he passes the bar he owes almost a quarter of a million bucks and he's lucky if he gets a job starting at a law firm for around $30 grand. Meanwhile another kid puts off college while he signs up as an apprentice in one of the trade unions. He's making $25 bucks an hour as a bricklayer and in the next seven years he amasses a fortune as he forms his own construction company, gets into property development, and winds up hiring the law school chump to handle his real estate closings.

Not enough plumbers and bricklayers, that'll be the reason for the complete breakdown of our society. Sure there'll be plenty of lawyers suing each other but homes with toilets will be scarce and we'll all wind up stepping in each other's problems. And all those lawyers will be living in cardboard mansions patched together with duct tape by unskilled, untrained, non-union labor. But it's not too late to stop the madness.

Encourage your kids to work with their hands and consider a career as a craftsman. That doesn't make them dumbbells. There's a hell of a lot more math and science involved in bricklaying and plumbing than there is in a pair of legal briefs. There's nobility to the trades. The plumbers proudly call it their "honorable toil". Hey, Joseph and Mary encouraged <u>their</u> son to go into carpentry. It was good enough for Him!

NO SMALL PARTS

Irish American News
WBEZ Public Radio
October 1997

I was watching the movie "Donnie Brasco" at home the other night and the end of the film was spoiled for me by a flamboyant extra.

The Feds had grabbed Pacino and were handcuffing him as they pulled Donnie Brasco away and Al screamed, "Don't tell 'em nothin', Donny!"

The camera panned back to Donnie's reaction shot as he's led up the dock ramp and suddenly this guy wearing an FBI jacket prances through the frame, waving his gun like he was auditioning for a community theatre production of Swan Lake.

I rewound the tape and watched the scene over again. The guy had only been on the screen for about five seconds but that was all it took for this law n' order Liberace to destroy the scene. He didn't even say anything, just sort of minced down the gangplank like he was looking for the drapery department at Fields.

That's just an example of how important every role in a movie can be. I thought of this recently when I was asked to audition for another movie as a cop with only one line. Over the last few years I've developed a somewhat besmirched reputation as a one-line specialist in film shot in Chicago.

I was the cop in the liquor store who wrestled Halle Berry to the ground and handcuffed her in "Losing Isaiah"; right after asking her, "Where's the party?"

I'm the tow truck driver who laughed in Juliana Margulies face in an episode of "ER".

My witty rejoinder as the hot dog vendor in "Rookie of the Year" wound up on the cutting room floor.

But I've been featured in several episodes of "Early Edition" as the bartender with brilliant variations of "What'll it be?"

Probably the best one line I've had to call my own was "Get the f—— outta here!" in the straight-to-video production of "Henry, Portrait of Serial Killer, Part II".

Once again I was the bartender and they called upon my seasoned expertise to usher our anti-hero out the door. I didn't even have to audition.

The director pulled me aside while we were setting up and asked me, "Are you from the Southside?"

"Yeah, that's right!" I replied proudly.

"Can't you cut it back on the accent?"

"What accent?"

I started out doing one-liners in Shakespeare in the early days of my career. I was the leader of a group of soldiers in MACBETH and we marched out of a pit in middle of the stage. MacDuff would give our squadron an order and I triumphantly exclaim, "It shall done!"

I tried underplaying it, throwing it away, shouting it, whispering it, using a Scottish accent, everything. Finally the director screamed at me, "What the hell are you doing? Just say it and get off!" I took that as good advice then and still practice it today.

As I was leaving the stage, one of the older Shakespearean thespians pulled me aside and draped his arm over my shoulder. "Remember luv, there are no small parts, there are only small actors!" Then he pinched me on the butt and walked onstage for his entrance.

Take a look at those guys playing the butler next time you're watching a flick. They were standing around all day and all last night staring into the mirror saying, "Dinner is served."

And they still get their own private dressing room; make several hundred bucks for the day, and free food as long as they're on the set. What a great business.

I guess my appreciation of "under fives' as they're called in show biz, is that while you may not say much, you still have the ability to screw up the whole picture. That's a big responsibility. Just think of the guy playing the jury foreman who can't keep a straight face saying, "Not Guilty, your honor." and you'll know what I'm talking about.

"We cannot all be great, but some of us can be part of something that is great." Let's hope so anyway. Nobody brags about being in a turkey. But you can be sure the guy who played the waiter in "The Godfather" is proud as hell. He's the little Italian guy who displays the bottle of wine to Commissioner McCloskey, and Salazzo in the restaurant before Michael Corleone whacks them. The guy was perfect!

So, maybe the guy in "Donnie Brasco" was trying something different? Maybe he was <u>trying</u> to look like Michael Jackson at a Boy Scout meeting. That's one way to get people asking your name. It becomes the immediate answer to that age old question, "Who is that schmuck?"

And let's not forget that some of the world's greatest actors started out in movies playing waiters. The scene at the Chez Paul when Elwood and Jake are ordering dinner in "The Blues Brothers?" The waiter is none other than the notoriously brilliant Pee Wee Herman. And we all know what happened to him!

BAD COMPANY

Irish American News
WBEZ Public Radio
November 1997

I come from a long line of black sheep.

I thought of this recently when sportscaster Marv Albert finally admitted his guilt as a weirdo. I have no sympathy for Marv, lock him up. But I started wondering how his brothers must feel now that Marv has shamed the Albert name. Marv has at least two younger brothers who are also sportscasters and I doubt if there are any ladies undergarments in their wardrobe.

That doesn't mean that female co-workers will be any less apprehensive when one of Marv's brothers asks her if she'd like to join him for a bite to eat. The news about Marv's kinky predilections shouldn't impede his brothers from doing their job, but it will. The audience will gasp each time one of them cries out, "He shoots, he scores!"

I guess it's been like that for brothers throughout history. Talk about sibling rivalry. It's one thing to live in the shadow of a more famous brother, but when he's a world-renowned villain your chances of gainful employment plummet. How would you like to be Geoff Dahmer's little brother? Sure all the neighbors remember kind lil' Ernie Dahmer. "Nice kid, easygoing, ... I think he was an altar boy. But his brother was a cannibal!"

And how about that creep from Hell, Richard Speck. No brothers, but I heard somewhere he had a sister who was very fond of him. Some guy actually fell in love with and married her, but as his head hits the pillow each night for the last thirty years he still can't help but wonder, "How did I wind up married into the Speck family!"

If you come from a large family I'm sure you have all polled each other on the psychological quirks of your siblings. Maybe Marv Albert's brothers knew he was a ticking bomb and they saw it coming. It started back in seventh grade when little Marv would filch his sister's bloomers.

We don't get together every Thanksgiving and speculate on who in our family could be the next national nutcase. But sometimes I feel like they're waiting for me to run naked through the next fancy political fundraiser. Certainly I've thought about it, but who hasn't? Come on, I haven't done anything like that in years. But that look of wary caution is always in their eyes when I'm visiting, as if I would suddenly bolt through the kitchen smashing things and somehow wind up on the cover of the National Enquirer.

Any one of my five brothers has the potential to spring a leak in the brain bathtub. But they still insist that I'm the one with water damage. Last Christmas my brother Johnny leaned over his Old Bushmills and sneered at me, "How do you think Adolph's brother Bob felt? Sure he's a nice guy, but he's known forever as a Hitler!"

And I have to admit he's right. If you're making a nice buck with a Beantown fishing show as the Boston Angler, you're bound to be bitter when your brother Al turns out to be the Boston Strangler. While my brothers seem poised for my unraveling, I'm just as ready for any one of them to cry havoc. I'll kindly greet them as they're lead away in a straitjacket and tell them tenderly how happy I was to pave the way for them.

So with the holiday season approaching let's all remember the potential Marvs, Adolph's, and Als in our families. Make it a point to buy them a drink and let them know you care. Because one of these years you might not be seeing them anymore. They could be dead, or in jail, or visiting the nuthouse, or the next RuPaul.

Black sheep are still your family. Tragic, embarrassing, or wacko, you've got to tough it out. You've got to remember the good times, and forget about the baaaa....baaaaa...aaaaaaaad.

MANHATTAN SANTA

Irish American News
WBEZ Public Radio
December 1997

"Get outta that bed you bum, you're playing Santa Claus today!"

These tender words were whispered in my ear by my wife one December morn back in the early eighties. I had spent the previous night at a Christmas party at O'Donnell's bar in Times Square. Pete Dooley the bartender, Eddie the stagehand, old deaf John and a couple of cops from the local precinct had been whooping it up in our local Hell's Kitchen hangout. Night people. We had been warbling "Oh Holy Night" til four am and the hookers on Eighth Avenue said we sounded great.

I had been relieved of my duties that day as early morning porter at the bar by Pete's cousin Pat because of my shoddy workmanship in cleaning out the urinals each morning. After six months of opening O'Donnells every morning at six am, mopping the floor, stocking the beer coolers, and occasionally scrubbing the toilets, I was fired. Pat had called me that night and asked me to stop by the bar and "bring your keys." The jig was up and I knew it. Once I started avoiding the scrubbing and tried to cover my tracks by filling the urinals with ice each morning it was only a matter of time before they smelled a rat.

O'Donnell's had stood at 43rd and Eighth Avenue for over fifty years and that venerable clan also operated Gaelic Park in the Bronx forever. I was proud to be their porter. Prouder still to have keys to the bar, especially when I would walk by on a Sunday night after they'd closed and I'd invite my friends in for a nightcap. It was only sixty bucks a week but the job had perks.

There were no hard feelings Pat explained, it was just those damned urinals had to be sparkling and I had fallen down on the job. "But Pat, it's Christmas!", I exclaimed. "Yeah, I know, we hired a college kid, here have a drink, Merry Christmas."

And so I had celebrated my demise and my liberation from the urinals that night. Celebrated too much. My lovely Mary reminded me that I was due at the Head Start program that morning because I had volunteered to play Santa for the kids. Just the antidote for a stinko hangover, hundreds of screaming brats yanking at my fake beard.

There was no talking my way out of it because two of those kids were mine. I could just imagine them coming home and telling me, "Yeah Santa Claus was a no show, they said he was sleepin' off a bender."

So I grabbed my coat and faced the biting wind as I trudged down 42nd street towards my doom. The tears from my eyeballs had turned to icicles by the time I crawled up the steps to the school just a block and a half away.

Jerry, the overly earnest school administrator, greeted me as he ushered me into his office and laid out the Santa suit. "This is going to be so much fun, you're the perfect Santa!" The booze was boiling in my gut and I could feel the blood vessels in my face expanding as I bent down to tie the black shiny boots. The "old" part of my performance would be easy, but I had my doubts about being "jolly".

"Where's the pillow for my stomach?"

"I don't think you need one, Santa!"

Jerry plied me with black coffee as he explained the routine. There were presents for every kid marked with their names in my bag and I would hand them out, pass out some oranges and cookies, sing some songs with the kids, lots of ho-ho-ho's, the standard tawdry charade.

I swung the bag over my shoulder and headed for the classrooms. "Santa can't stay long boys and girls." I thought to myself, "He just might have to make a mad dash for the North Pole bathroom at any minute!"

Outside the door I paused for a moment to psych myself up. My Santa beard had an odor I could not identify and I was trying to breathe through my mouth only. I could barely hear them on the other side of the door as I placed my white-gloved mitt on the knob and swung it open. "Ho, ho, ho, Merry Christmas!"

Pandemonium! Little girls shrieking "Santa" as they spun around the room like whirling dervishes; awestruck four year olds staring at me as if I was the burning bush; and wise guy towheads with their hands in their pockets, anxiously wondering if I knew about that booger they wiped on Sally and was I carrying any lumps of coal for them. I instantly felt infused with the power of Santa Claus and threw myself into the performance.

I planted a big smooch on the gorgeous kindergarten teacher and started handing out the presents. Their innocence, excitement, and joy were infectious and all of a sudden I felt like a million bucks. As we sang "Rudolph the Red-nosed Reindeer", a scrawny little guy plopped onto my lap and peeled his orange with the only three fingers on his right hand. He was different, just like Rudolph, but today he belonged. He was with his old pal Santa and the teachers told me later that those presents might be the only ones some of those kids would get for Christmas.

Sure it's corny, but I've always been a sucker for that old Christmas feelin'. I was no longer worried about losing my job as the Porter of the Pissoir. Hey, that's nothing; I had a better job, Santa Claus for cripesakes! I anxiously awaited the arrival of my boys after school to quiz them on my performance.

"Hey, how was school today?"

"It was great! Santa Claus was there!"

"Yeah, Dad, he even knew our names!"

"Was he acting real jolly?"

"Yeah, he was really jolly, and he smelled like beer!"

CHAPTER TWO

1998

ST. VALENTINE

Irish American News
WBEZ Public Radio
February 1998

The Catholic Church removed St. Valentine from the calendar way back in 1969. We never heard about this because the greeting card, floral, and candy industry made sure we didn't. The name Saint Valentine is given to two legendary Christian martyrs whose feasts were formerly observed on February 14. One was believed to be a Roman priest martyred around 269 AD and the other was a bishop martyred in Rome. It's possible that these two legends were based on real people, but the association of Saint Valentine with love and courtship probably arose from the coincidence of the date of the Roman festival of Lupercalia.

Evidently the Vatican felt that there wasn't enough clear information about this guy Valentine. The history is vague as to who he was and there are even a couple of theories that he was a combination of the two guys. There were plenty of people who wanted to credit St. Valentine with miracles, but after careful investigation it was determined that the same types of miracles were occurring through the use of flowers, candy, and sweetalk anyway and they never involved the invocation of a saint.

Actually I'm surprised that the floral greeting card industry didn't do its homework. I've done a little research on this and discovered some very interesting background on a guy named Valentine Mostaccioli in Rome back in the third century. His dad owned a chariot repair shop and young Val didn't seem to have an aptitude for school, so the old man put him to work as a chauffeur. So Val was the only kid in the neighborhood who had constant access to wheels. This was a pretty heady status symbol for young Romans in those days and Val was a pretty slick operator. He had a different chariot every night of the week that his dad would let him zip around town in and this of course attracted plenty of young Roman gals.

The rest of the Roman youth were understandably jealous of Val, but what could they do? They'd see him every Friday night at the Gladiator matches with two or three gorgeous gals in tight togas on his arm and they would assume he had a certain charm and that's why the ladies were smitten. And Val of course played right into the image as a ladies man. He had plenty of gold chains around his neck and would give the girls flowers that he picked from his aunt Sophia's garden.

It was very frustrating for the other young lads of Rome to see Val escorting all the eligible females down the Apian Way and finally they elected a spokesman, Houlihanus, to speak to Val about it.

"Hey, Val, what's the deal with all the chicks?", he asked the swarthy chariot jockey.

"Yo, Houlihanus, what can I tell ya, it's a gift. Treat 'em right and they'll love ya for it."

"But you're the only dude in town with a chariot. How can we compete when you've got a corner on all the fine enchiladas?"

And that's when Val discovered the commerce of romance.

"I will rent you my old man's chariot for twenty drachmas a night. Here's another clue, Houlihanus, try bathing more than once a fortnight and the women might find you more stimulating."

This sounded like good advice to Houlihanus and he passed these words of wisdom on to the rest of the Roman lads. After awhile they began to rely on Valentine's guidance in getting along with the opposite sex. He told them to shower the girls with chocolate covered cannoli, flowers from his Aunt Sophia's garden, and every once in awhile "drop her a note tellin' her how she has captured your heart or something! Dat really drives 'em wild!"

And the next thing you know all the lads of Rome were squiring the ladies all over town in Val's chariots, and giving them candy and flowers and love notes. And it worked, Val was right, the ladies loved it. The lads of Rome were very appreciative of Val's advice and were even heard to remark, "That Valentine, man, he saved my life with the dollies, he is a saint!"

But the night before the feast of Lupercalia, Valentine made a blunt announcement.

"The price of the chariot rides is double tomorrow, and the chocolate covered cannoli is now gonna cost you fifteen drachmas a box, and the flowers from my aunt Sophia's garden is twenty drachmas, and I want two bucks a piece to write them mushy love notes."

And Houlihanus and the rest of the Roman youth said, "Hey, what gives?"

And Val said, "Supply and demand baby, besides my aunt Sophie is gonna ring my neck over all dem flowers we took, so I gotta pay her off. So meet me tonight at my old man's garage and you better bring drachmas or there will be a severe shortage of female entertainment at the feast of Lupercalia this year."

When the Roman lads showed up that night at Val's garage, they made him an offer he couldn't refuse. And that night on the eve of the feast of Lupercalia in 269 AD was the original St. Valentine's Day Massacre.

KEN'S

Irish American News
WBEZ Public Radio
April 1998

I don't think Robert Goulet has ever been to the Southside of Chicago. There is a unique form of etiquette that is practiced in the bars and drinking establishments on Western Avenue and apparently the Canadian matinee idol is not familiar with this code. His ignorance in this matter probably resulted in one of the most humiliating nights of his career, second only to the time he forgot the words to the National Anthem in mid-song before one of the heavyweight championship bouts in Las Vegas. It was yet another example of that age-old maxim, "Don't open your mouth if you don't know the deal."

I was having a beer in Ken's on Western Avenue, probably my favorite watering hole, on the Southside a few months ago and the TV was blaring a basketball game. Robert Goulet suddenly appeared on the tube doing a commercial or something and the entire bar began hurling insults and invective in the direction of the Zenith on the wall. The room instantly transformed itself into an angry mob whose sole purpose was to vilify Goulet. There were even some nasty remarks made about his ex-wife Carol Lawrence, most of them having to do with her upbringing in Melrose Park.

The communal harangue ended just as suddenly as it began when the idiot box switched back to the game. I was puzzled by this mass critique of a fellow thespian and curious as to how Goulet could trigger such a negative response. "What's the deal with Robert Goulet?", I asked Jimmy Heffernan as I sidled onto the vacant stool to his left. He chortled as he nodded in the direction of our host, the greatest bartender in the city of Chicago, Jack Casto. I've known Jackie since we were nippers and our Dads were best pals. My old man would decorate the mahogany of Sam Casto's joint at 89th and Loomis back in the good old days. Jack Casto and I would tag along with our pops and wait for the change to fall out of their pockets when they had a load on.

So I can attest to Jack's buoyant personality behind the bar, but I'll also be the first to tell you that you don't want to be on Jackson's bad side. And Robert Goulet had taken up permanent residence there since the "incident" in Indianapolis. It seems that Hef and Casto were out in Indy for somebody's third cousin's wedding and they were having a cocktail in the hotel bar the day after the shindig. Goulet was on tour in CAMELOT and walked into the bar with his entourage of sycophants from the show. As he passed Casto and Hef he stopped to make what he thought was a funny remark about Jack's sweater. This unsolicited critique of Casto's clothes was Goulet's undoing.

The first words out of Jack's mouth were of course unprintable. So were the second, third, fourth, fifth, sixth, and well you get the idea. He spun around on his stool to confront this Broadway Beau Brummel and unleashed the full fury of a Southside of Chicago challenge in Goulet's puffy face. It was time to "exit, stage left" for the Canadian and he began backpedaling his Beatle boots toward the hotel lobby.

But Jackie was on the offensive now, castigating his wardrobe, his wife, his phony friends, and especially his recently lackluster career as he followed

Goulet out into the lobby, flinging contempt and scorn in his path. The hotel guests stood awestruck as all action stopped in the lobby and they watched Robert Goulet run for the elevators to escape the wrath of Jack Casto. As the doors closed for his getaway, Jackie hurled one more grenade in Goulet's direction as he sneered at the top of his lungs, "Go back to Camelot, you're nothin' but a phony, two-bit, broken-down, has-been, actor!"

Ouch! So much for Robert Goulet's introduction to the niceties of the Southside of Chicago. He had just received a free trip down Western Avenue and never had to set foot in the windy city. And he continues to live in infamy whenever his mug happens to appear on the tube in Ken's. But of course he asked for it, walking up to a total stranger and trying to amuse his coterie of flatterers by ridiculing Jack Casto's fashion sense.

Last I heard the gang at Ken's was forming a fan club for Goulet. They're hoping to interest him in bringing a show out to the Southside. It won't be Camelot, after all that's just a fairy tale. But I think they'd be thrilled to see "Bob" in a musical version of DEAD MAN WALKING.

SPECIAL INTENTIONS

Irish American News
WBEZ Public Radio
June 1998

At my parish, St. Luke's, the priest asks the congregation at weekday masses to add their own personal requests during the Prayers of the Faithful. People usually say things like, "For my uncle Bob who is having surgery this morning, let us pray to the Lord." And the congregation answers with "Lord Hear our Prayer." It's a nice touch and thankfully his nephew did not inform us that Uncle Bob was having hemorrhoid surgery. That would be too personal. Too much information.

But the other day I must admit I wanted to throw a prayer out there for Ol' Blues, "For the repose of the soul of the Chairman of the Board, Frank Sinatra". But I chickened out at the last minute for fear I would upset the unwritten rules of decorum for personal intentions.Because I'm sure if we all knew what everybody else was praying for there would be mild outrage and accusations of taking advantage of the power of group prayer.

I always feel that having the whole church behind me on a prayer has got to carry more weight with God than just my lonely old voice calling out in the wilderness. So I'll say something like, "For a special intention, let us pray to the Lord." when I'm actually praying to win Lotto that weekend. Well actually not Lotto, but a quick way to bail me out of tapioca with some cold, hard, cash, please God.

And it works. I may not always get exactly what I'm praying for, but I invariably find a way out of my particular dilemma. The Lord always draws a straight line but sometimes he uses a crooked stick. That's me, the crooked stick. And just as soon as I get myself out of one jam with the aid of the St. Luke congregation praying behind me, I always seem to find myself in another one before too long. I guess that's God's way of keeping me praying. It's not like a bank where they shut you off after you've borrowed so much dough. No, these prayers are like a bank that will just keep on handing it over. It would be a ridiculous way to run a real business, but I guess that's why it's spiritual, anything and everything is possible.

So I usually throw reasonable stuff out there, all under the umbrella of "a special intention", safety and prosperity for my kids, another good thirty years until I kick the bucket, and maybe that basketball pool at the office for a quick 500 bucks. Hey, it's just between the Lord and me so what's the problem?

Well my problem is I'm sometimes tempted to verbally throw one out there for guys like Frank Sinatra, the Mt. Carmel hockey team, or the complete disintegration of the Internal Revenue Service. Now these all seem like reasonable intentions to me that would be near and dear to the heart of Our Lord, but maybe not the rest of my partners in the pews.

I remember a lady last year asking for a prayer for "Baby Richard", a kid involved in a custody battle between his birth parents and some yuppies that adopted him. Her prayer was no doubt sincere for the welfare of the child, but I somehow felt she had been reading a little too much Bob Greene in the Tribune and his maudlin whining had influenced her request. I restrained myself from turning around and giving her a dirty look and asking, "What next? A prayer for the poor woman who was recently abducted by aliens and featured on the cover of the National Enquirer?"

Certainly my response would not have been very Christian, but it also made me aware that while we are all praying together, we may not all share the same viewpoint on the recipients of our prayers. While I may think that "A speedy recovery from the flu for Minnie Minoso", is a legitimate request, someone else may feel that I am trivializing their celestial energy as a group. So I've learned to keep my mouth shut and just say, "For a special intention."

And you hear a lot of them at my church. That's part of the intrigue of the service for me, not knowing <u>exactly</u> what we're all praying for, but knowing that whatever it may be, we are all chipping in to help deliver those ultimately good intentions for each of us. Those "special intentions" provide a flavor of the spiritual mystery that has been so sorely missed since the changeover from the Latin mass. It just seemed holier then. Sure we only had a vague idea of what we were saying, but hey, that can be very mysterious.

So here's to the special intention. It's a catchall, which cloaks your politics, persuasion, or poverty, but never your purity of heart. So go ahead and say one for Frank Sinatra, Mayor Daley, or even (God forbid) Jerry Reinsdorf, but keep it under your hat with the "special intention'. And hey, while you're at it, please, say one for me!

PUT A CORK IN IT

Irish American News
WBEZ Public Radio
August 1998

I found out recently that the new miracle drug Viagra is being manufactured in Cork, Ireland. I'm sure this bodes well for the economic resurgence of the old country and potency of our Celtic Tiger. But I'm not so sure this new industry will benefit the image of the "terrible beauty" as a chaste country.

While France, Germany, and certainly Greece have been known for centuries for their liberal attitudes concerning sex; Ireland has remained a wholesome and modest nation with a healthy, though somewhat provincial outlook on sex. Heaven knows the Irish are certainly doing it, just look at the size of our families. But thankfully we have kept our bedroom antics appropriately a private matter. Holy Mother Church is probably responsible for this discretion but it's also one of the contributing factors to the unquestionable dignity of our race.

When Sean O' Casey's epic Irish drama, THE PLOUGH AND THE STARS, debuted in Dublin many years ago, the audiences were up in arms and riots occurred outside the theatre. One of the major causes of their consternation was the fact that O'Casey had dared to portray an Irish woman as a prostitute. While the crowd may have grudgingly acknowledged that two or three practitioners of this unfortunate trade actually existed in the Erin Isle, there certainly was no reason to tell the world. "It's nobody's business but our own."

You won't find a sexier scene in Irish cinema than Duke Wayne planting a passionate kiss on Maureen O'Hara as the rain washed across her ravishing features and scarlet locks in "The Quiet Man". It was mysterious, sensual, and we didn't need to know more. And then they got married. That's the way it's supposed to be.

But this Viagra factory in Cork has the potential to corrupt all that. First of all I'm not sure the product would sell in Ireland because no self-respecting Irishman would ever admit to needing a jump-start.

And once this capsule of carnality is unleashed on our ancestral home, who knows what depths of depravity may lie ahead? I can just imagine Irish porno being bootlegged out of the Ol' Sod starring freckle faced Seamus Shillelagh in "Deidre Drops Her Drawers".

And what about that old custom, still in practice at the Guinness brewery, which entitles each worker to an allotment of free samples each week? I don't think ol' Bridget will be too thrilled with the Viagra company's largesse when she finds out what Pat is bringing home. I can just see the scene at their kitchen table before she discovers what his new job entails.

Bridget: "And so how's the new job goin' Paddy?"

Pat: "Grand, Bridget, didn't they give me some free samples to take home with me."

Bridget: "Free samples, is it? Well don't be hidin' them like ya used to do with the Guinness now. We'll have it with our dinner tonight. Get it out and get it on the table."

Pat: "Ahh, you're a darlin' girl, Bridget!"

Before you know it, the city of Cork will be the newest member of a tri-umvirate that includes Sodom and Gomorra. The pubs will be empty and "Irish hospitality" will take on a whole new meaning for the tourist trade when eighty-year-old Barry Fitzgerald types start thinking like Hugh Hefner. Once the leprechauns get their hands on this stuff they'll no longer be known as the "little people". Impotent geezers all over the world will be urged by advertisers to "put a cork in it."

Over the years Ireland's greatest export has been our wit, whiskey, and wisdom. Let's not desecrate the romantic memory of Ireland by sending synthetic whoopee across the Irish Sea. We've enough to be proud of without pushing Burger King aside for claims to the dubious distinction of the home of the Whopper.

Unless of course we could copyright it. Not so much for the money, but the satisfaction of knowing that Eire once again has unleashed on the world a product of creativity and spirit that could benefit all mankind; much like our poetry, music, and laughter. Let's start negotiating trade tariffs which stipulate that each and every "miracle" resulting from this wonder drug be emblazoned with a green tattoo proclaiming the three words that warm the cockles of every Irish-American's heart, "Made In Ireland".

OLEG CASSINI

Irish American News
November 1998

People often ask me what is the most memorable event I've experienced in my amazing life. Was it the sight of Tom Tuite, my old college roommate, heaving-at-will in the cafeteria? Or was it the time that Dogs Daugherty drank beer through his nostrils in sophomore year in high school? Could it have been the time we watched the members of the Ladies Altar Guild Society from Christ The King parish change into their bathing suits as we spied from a knothole in the back of Beverly Country Club's pool?

Well, while those aforementioned thrills certainly have done a great deal in establishing my reputation as an international adventurer, I must admit that probably one of the most memorable events in my notorious career was the night I met Oleg Cassini.

Yes, Oleg Cassini, the international fashion designer and playboy. He had dated Grace Kelley and Jackie Onassis and a long list of high-class bimbos over the years and you probably own a tie or scarf designed by him. His career had long since hit it's apex when I met him in the early eighties but he was still the biggest shot I had ever met up with and I want to tell you I was impressed. I just happened to be wearing one of his sport coats the night we met.

I was between jobs at the time, suffering from an acute case of Tapioca, as in Tap City, Tapped Out, Tapioca. A fly-by-night film producer by the name of Bradley Wolfington was trying to raise money for a movie that was already shot and in the can. He offered me a piece of the pie if I could bring in any investors for this fiasco.

"Well I gotta see the movie first, see if I can sell it."

"No problem," says Bradley, 'I'm having' a private screening tonight at the Borg Warner Building. Be there at eight."

So I put on my blazer and tie and I'm there. I'm the only guy in this screening room that seats about sixty people and I'm thinking, "This Bradley is really a mope if he set this whole thing up for me, I mean, I'm tapioca!"

And in walks this gorgeous French babe on the arm of a tall, distinguished looking guy, in a double-breasted blazer, silver hair and mustache. They look like they've just stepped out of the centerfold of Vogue magazine and they saunter down the aisle and plop down right in front of me. She's cooing in his ear and he's doing that French guy laugh, even though he's from Italy. "Honh...honh...honh. "

I finally interrupt their foreplay to inquire if he is the one and only Oleg Cassini and they are both very friendly and yes he is, and she is Suzette, and

I'm Mike and what a coincidence that I am wearing an Oleg Cassini sport coat that I bought off the rack at St. Malachy's Thrift Shop.

"So are you guys going to invest in the movie?" I ask nosily.

"Perhaps Michele, we shall see"

So I tell them, "Yeah, perhaps me too, I just wanna see if it's the kind of thing that would be worthy of the Oleg Cassini influence." And she says, "Bravo Michele!" just as the lights go down and the movie starts up.

Five minutes into the screening and I can tell that this film is the worst piece of dog crap I've ever seen. The plot involves a bunch of sorority sisters in a house being terrorized by an axe-wielding psychopath. Sound familiar? It's got lots of bra and panty shots, bad acting, fuzzy picture, bad lighting, blood all over the place, and even the screams are out of synch. And the whole thing is in German!

Well I figure this has got to be a joke, right? So I start to laugh at some of this ridiculous cinema noir and Oleg joins in.

"Honh....honh...honh!"

Sure, it's a very sophisticated attempt at a parody of the old' sorority house, panty and bra, thriller, genre, thing.

And Suzette says, "Oui Michele, merde, merde!"

So the lights come up and bozo Bradley comes out and stands in front of the screen. "Well folks, whadja think?"

We ask Bradley why it's in German and he tells us he just needs a little cash to dub it into English and get in the theaters and start figuring out what we're going to do with all that dough we're gonna make. He tells Suzette that he never thought of it as a comedy, "But hell, that might work too!"

We all turn to Oleg for his expert opinion on matters foreign and fashionable and he leans back in his seat, crosses his legs with aplomb and a pair of Italian loafers made from the skin of a young duckling and no socks, and pronounces Bradley's film, "Trash!"

Bradley seems unfazed, "Of course it is. But it's trash that could make you a lot of moolah!"

Oleg bolts from his seat, with Suzette in tow, and turns at the door and delivers the following line as if he was challenging Bradley to a bullfight or something, "Sir, do not make a fool of me!"

My pal Oleg

It sounded really cool the way he said it too, sort of that vaguely foreign accent in conjunction with his head held high as he let the word, "Fooooool", drip with contempt from his noble mouth. Pure class, and then he turns on his heel and exits with panache and the sound of Suzette's high heels clicking across the floor behind him.

That was the last time I saw Oleg. I was kind of hoping that we would become pals and hang out in tony New York cocktail lounges with Suzette and nibble caviar. But even though our paths never crossed again I am forever in his debt because he showed me how to turn an ugly situation into a dignified event.

I used it just the other day when I was bowling with Dogs Daugherty and I caught him cheating and trying to get me to pay for the final beer frame. I leapt from my seat, threw my bowling shoes, (made from the skin of a young tender Nauga), onto the lane, and stood in my stocking feet on the top step, and said, "Sir, you dirty *%#@!!!, do not make a fooooool of me!"

HOLIDAY NUTS

Irish American News
WBEZ Public Radio
December 1998

Holiday preparations at my house when I was a kid growing up included not only decorating the tree and shopping for gifts but also getting the family ready for the nuts. Not the walnuts or cashews my mom would put out in a bowl on the coffee table but the nuts of my parent's family. It seemed like every Thanksgiving and Christmas my folks would play host to one or other of their screwball siblings. It's a tradition that is repeated in homes across America today as families start discussing in early November who is going to take the wacko into their home on turkey day. At our house we always alternated between my mom's psychotic sister Alice or my dad's boozy brother Paul.

On Christmas and New Years Day it would be a double header with both Alice and Paul showing up to put on the feedbag. We looked forward to it as kids because our parents let both Alice and Paul get away with behavior that ordinarily would be forbidden in our house. Aunt Alice smoked and

Uncle Paul got blasted and told great stories with lots of swearing and crude references to various ethnic groups, all of whom he nicknamed "Harvey".

My mom's sister Alice was divorced and in those days that meant she was destined to go directly to hell. But what did she expect when she married a Protestant? That was the subtle lesson my mom hoped had been learned by us kids as we discussed the foibles of Aunt Alice before her annual entrance.

Poor Alice was very high strung and nervous as a result of her failed marriage. We could never get the whole story out of my mom, only that Alice's ex was also named Harvey and was definitely not Irish.

The shock of her wedding night with Harvey had turned her hair bright white and she always looked skinny and surprised. Even though she was only in her late forties then she seemed to us like the proverbial crazy old lady as she smoked her L&M's, sipped her bourbon and ginger, and would constantly be exclaiming her wonderment over the holiday feast with her signature rhetorical expression that us kids thought was hilarious, "Isn't this the berries?"

Uncle Paul was the oldest and the only bachelor of the three Houlihan brothers who grew up on Root Street on the Southside. He was a retired Chicago cop and he was the breadwinner for my Dad and Uncle Frank when they were orphaned in their teens.

He lived in a boarding house and would always bring his pal Mister Sullivan with him. "Sully" as we were allowed to call him as we fetched booze and pretzels, was another retired cop who lived in the boarding house and played sort of a Stan Laurel to Uncle Paul's Oliver Hardy.

Uncle Paul would hold court in our living room, squatting back in the best chair and crack us up with funny stories of all the "Harveys" whose heads he had busted on the Southside over the years. Sully would never say a word, just perched there chuckling and drinking, with his lanky legs crossed and his long underwear sticking out of his pants legs, as he awaited the shot of the starters pistol for dinner.

My mom used to make two turkeys when Sully and Uncle Paul visited. Sully may have looked scrawny but the guy was like a pit bull around that gravy boat, and Uncle Paul was no slouch either.

This was our "company" every holiday season. I don't know if the tradition was more fun for them or for us. When you're a kid every adult who is not your mom or dad seems eccentric. But then you discover that sharing the holiday with your crazy aunts and uncles and cousins is what made it special. It made our family seem not only bigger that day, but maybe a little brighter as well.

And we always had that smug satisfaction as we watched the cab taking them away at the end of the night that our family was the most normal of them all. Until we became adults of course. Then we discovered the idiosyncrasies of our own family.

And every holiday season we introduce our kids to their wacky aunts and uncles, as each generation will hopefully continue to do with theirs. And we all sooner or later discover that nobody is as peculiar as we once thought they were.

I visited Aunt Alice a few years ago right before she died out at St. Joseph's Home for the elderly in Palatine. It was their summer picnic and I had my kids with me and we all played bingo under the tent. Alice was smoking Newports now and drinking a beer and seemed as normal as Bloomington. I could swear she hadn't changed a bit, except that she thought my twins were "Mike". And when the lady next to us shouted out "Bingo", Alice turned to us and said, "Isn't this the berries?"

Uncle Paul died while I was living out of town. He had started spending his winters in Mexico when I was in my twenties, so I hadn't seen him in years.

My dad had received a Christmas card one year from him with a photo of Uncle Paul and Sully, seated by the pool in bathing suits drinking pina coladas and the inscription, "Merry Christmas, it just ain't the same without Harvey."

Sully looked ridiculous without his long underwear but Uncle Paul looked very comfortable with his new beard and fat belly. Santa Claus in a speedo.

So this holiday season make sure you have all the required accouterments: the holly, the tree, the turkey, the pumpkin pie, and if you want to make it a Christmas they'll always remember, don't forget the nuts.

CHAPTER THREE
1999

HOOPLES

Irish American News
March 1999

Oprah was jabbering about some goo- goo garbage on the tube when Arnie opened his eyes. She can make a buck just by belching. He peered into the smoky tin tiles of the ceiling and turned up his eario.

A kid with a mop was knocking around his feet in the booth where he lay and Arnie Murphy stiffened into a sitting position. Still got my clothes on. Where am I?

Deja vu. The Gate of Heaven bar, his favorite Western Avenue watering hole. He squinted up at the tube in the corner and caught a whiff of his own well-earned stink. Nobody here but the kid and an empty bar.

Arnie turned to his left and got a good blast of March sunshine screaming into his eyeballs from the window on the street. He heard the kid shout, "He's up Mickey." as he walked toward the back and then the sound of Mickey Fogarty's shoes shuffling down the bar. Mickey looked tired and pissed as he snatched one of the crepe paper leprechauns hanging from the ceiling, cracked open a beer, slammed it on the mahogany, and sneered at Arnie.

"You screwy bastard. You put on a real wing ding of a show last night pal, I already deducted the cost of the broken mirror out of the poke in your pocket while you were sawin' logs."

"I broke a mirror?"

"Not you, Angela O'Reardon, when she bounced that shot glass off your head. Geesh, it's still swelled up, you got a nice egg on your forehead Arnie, you stinkin' hoople!"

Arnie sat dazed as he felt the bump on his head and measured Mickey's anger. "Sorry Mickey, I'm kind of inna fog right now. Must've blacked out."

"That's what hooples do on St. Patrick's Day."

"Wha, what's a hoople?"

"A hoople is a guy who goes on a rip roaring toot on Paddy's Day and comes in here three sheets to the wind, insults every customer in the joint, singin' Danny Boy off key, gooses the O'Reardon twins, picks a fight with grandpa Nolan, passes out in my booth and doesn't wake up til Oprah's on the next morning."

"The O'Reardon twins? From St. Cajetan's?"

"Yeah, they looked pretty hot last night, Erin Go Braless for St. Patrick's Day. But only a hoople would take that 'Kiss Me, I'm Irish' garbage as far as you did."

"What in the hell is a hoople?"

"You Arnie, you are a hoople. Hooples are guys who don't get served here anymore. I got a list of them right here behind the bar, Jimmy the goof, Ed Pishtarski from Hedgewish, and ten or eleven other lost souls. And last night when you were bouncing around here goin' east on Ashland, I put your name on that list. It's been nice knowin' ya."

"No, something was wrong Mickey. I think somebody put something in my drink."

"Yeah, it's called alcohol, you moron. By the way, you're wife called here looking for ya.

Arnie squinted at the clock. "My wife? I never called her. Geesh I'm supposed to be at work now." The grim reality of his night of debauchery was starting to dawn on Arnie. "Oh man Mickey, I'm in trouble. I guess I've finally hit bottom."

"You passed bottom at about ten thirty last night Arnie. You are now an official hoople."

It had started at the St. Patrick's Day parade queen contest two weeks earlier. An Italian girl had been elected and it caused a commotion in ol' Plumbers Hall that reverberated onto the streets of Irish Chicago. The Mayor had supposedly made a wisecrack and a Tribune columnist had held his feet to the fire. A freak snowstorm had also hit that week and something threw the stars into alignment for a very strange St. Patrick's Day indeed.

Arnie had marched in both parades that year with his fellow workers from the Water Department. His thirst seemed unquenchable as he gargled Bushmills and Guinness washed down with Miller Lites. He had also broken his golden rule of never eating corned beef and cabbage more than three times in a week. A mystical Celtic voodoo had triggered a breakdown of Arnie and sent him on a roller coaster ride he would forever remember as the bender of '98.

Was it the Italian queen, the El Nino snowstorm, or the extra lob of horseradish he spread across his cabbage at each shamrock soiree he had crashed? Or was it the combination of all these evil omens, churning that feeling of foreboding in his gut? He had tried to tame his trepidation with heavy doses of aqua vitae only to awake two days later labeled as a hoople.

"For Gods sake Mickey you gotta help me, I'm in big trouble. Divorce, fired, and now a hoople! What should I do?"

"Better get down on your knees right now and start praying to the patron saint of hooples, St. Cyril. Today's his feast day, March 18th."

"Was he a hoople?"

"Hooples don't get to Heaven Arnie. Not much is known about St. Cyril really. But the story goes that when he got to Heaven, St. Peter called him into his office and said, 'I got good news and bad news for ya. The good news is that we're making you a saint, the bad news is that we gotta stick ya between the Micks and the Dagos, March 18th.' And ever since that day, poor stupid slobs like you have been asking him for help after you use St. Patrick's Day as an excuse to behave like an Amadon."

Arnie started a novena to St. Cyril that very minute. Tears streamed down his face as he drove home down Western Avenue. Begging St. Cyril to help him, help him from being a hoople.

Facing the music was tough, but he told his wife of the jealous Water Dept. worker who slipped him the Mickey Finn, the tainted horseradish, and the Italian Queen. And wasn't it wise not to drive through that snow and ice from last week after having a few drinks? And he told her of St. Cyril, the patron saint of Hooples, and how he was turning over a new leaf, and certainly his behavior was indefensible, but after all, it still wasn't as bad as what the President of the United States had done!

Arnie went to mass on St. Joseph's Day morning with his lovely wife Mary and wormed his way back into the family. His kids were told of the gigantic water main break in Berwyn and how their Dad had worked all night and all day to become the new flood stud. He didn't get fired from the Water Department. Alderman Eddie Burke was still his Chinaman. But he swore by St. Cyril and St. Joseph that St. Patrick's Day of 1999 he would no longer be considered among that decrepit pool of humanity known as hooples.

"Yeah, I'm gonna take it easy this St. Patrick's Day. Hey, that's amateur night anyway. Maybe I'll take in a show. I heard that GOIN' EAST ON ASHLAND over at the Ivanhoe is terrific."

Let Arnie Murphy's tale of woe be a warning to us all. Celebrate St. Patrick's Day with class and stop acting like an ass. And when the day is done, and you wake up feeling human for a change, then send one up to ol' St. Cyril. Thank him for that smiling face you see shaving in the mirror. Save the wearing of the green for March 17th and not around your gills on the feast day of St. Cyril, the patron saint of hooples.

THE POT OF GOLD AT THE END OF 'DA RAINBOW

Irish American News
WBEZ Public Radio
April 1999

I was lucky enough last month to be in both of Chicago's St. Patrick's Day parades. Sure I've marched before with various groups of beer fueled revelers but this was the first time I actually had my own float. I thought it would be a fun way to publicize my show GOIN' EAST ON ASHLAND which plays around town each St. Patrick's Day.

And by being in both parades I could hit all of Chicago's Irish American community, the north side Irish, the south side Irish, and the west Side Irish. There are no East Side Irish, that's all Polish and perch.

I didn't have any problem getting in the downtown parade. My friends at the Plumbers Local 130 gave me a great position and plenty of promotion when I passed by the reviewing stand. After all I've been pitching flamshooters for these guys on TV for the last five years in their commercials. They've been good to me. Didn't they arrange for myself and Plumbing Council Director Bob Ryan to have our pictures taken for an O'Brien's restaurant ad, as the co-stars of the Union Plumbers commercials? If you didn't see the ad, stop by O'Brien's on Wells street and you'll be sure to see my picture, mounted proudly among the plumbing fixtures in the mens room, directly over the urinal.

But the Southside parade committee were a bit more discerning in their admission process. They warned me that there would be absolutely no drinking of alcohol on my float in their parade on Sunday. Maybe they tell everybody this, but I couldn't help feeling that somehow my reputation had preceded me.

Certainly I'm better known on the Southside. That's where I grew up and had my first beer. And sure I've misbehaved on occasion like any other Southside goofball. As a matter of fact I've kind of made a career out of it. But that was years ago guys. These days I'm a pillar of the community and only get locked up for disorderly conduct when I'm demonstrating for a worthy cause, like fighting the ban on Happy Hours. So the Southside finally acquiesced and welcomed me back to their bosom. They let me join their parade and gave me a nice position, right behind the Clydesdales.

My twin sons were in from college that weekend and I informed them that instead of basking in the sun of Florida with all the spoiled rich kids on Spring Break; they would earn a few extra bucks freezing their keesters off with me in the parades. They didn't actually jump at the opportunity, but when I told them we would have a bullhorn on the float so they could yell obscenities at any of their friends along the parade route, they were in.

Saturday was overcast and cold for the downtown parade. We met our float at Wacker and Wells and it really looked cool. Lots of shamrocks and Irish flags and the logo from GOIN' EAST ON ASHLAND festooned our unit. We also had a very snazzy rainbow that arched over the center of the float and made a great perch for me to sit on, as we would ride down Dearborn Street and greet the Irish of Chicago.

Our parade order position was right behind a promotional float for a radio station featuring a shock jock named Mancow. Apparently this guy was too important to be on his float that day but he had sent his assistant, a very rotund, hairy creep who has the unfortunate moniker of "Turd". And after seeing him in action I can attest to the fact that the name fits.

As we pulled out into the line of procession I started ranting on the bullhorn and wishing all the folks along the parade route a Happy St. Patrick's Day. I made a pitch for my show and then, when I couldn't think of anything else to say, launched into my worst rendition of "Danny Boy".

Suddenly I noticed the people in the crowd were shouting at me. I lowered my bullhorn to listen and was somewhat nonplused by their shouts of "Gay Pride!" Well, fine, but what does that have to do with me? It was then I learned that the rainbow is now a symbol of the gay movement. That's right, a rainbow, just like the one I was currently sitting on, as it thrust out from between my legs. I wanted to shout, "No, no, it's for leprechauns, and pots of gold, and God invented it as a signal to Noah after the great flood. It has nothing to do with sodomy, not that there's anything wrong with that!"

But my marketing instincts kicked into gear as I bit my lip and opted for a more politically correct, "Right on!" After all, the title of my show GOIN' EAST ON ASHLAND, was a metaphor for a life of misdirection and maybe they thought it was a new gay comedy about lascivious leprechauns. Hey, let them think that. They'd find out soon enough, hopefully after they had purchased their tickets.

But the idea of riding down Western Avenue with the symbol for gay pride jutting from my loins on the float the next day on the Southside did not bode well. I could just imagine the ridicule and scorn that would be slung my way by my old bar buddies. It's not like there are any chapters of the Gay and Lesbian air force on the south side. One of the more charming aspects of life on the Southside is our political incorrectness. Maybe they were not as enlightened as I regarding the symbol of the rainbow. They probably didn't even know. Rainbows are certainly not the hot topic of conversation in most Western avenue bars.

And so we set out down Western Avenue with the same routine, hearty Irish greetings, waving to the crowd, some off-key Danny Boy, and above, all urgent exhortations to buy tickets for GOIN' EAST ON ASHLAND. And the crowd was great, not a crack was made about buggery. My sons and I were relieved as we hopped off the float at 115th street. The Southside had done itself proud and treated us with respect. Oh, sure there were the usual shouts of "Houli, you fat pig, that float is gonna sink!" But those were my friends.

We went directly to a post parade party at Skinny Sheahan's and when I told my pal John "The Head" Sheahan about the new symbolism of the rainbow, his eyebrows arched over his beer can as he chuckled through his Southside drawl, "Does Finian know?"

THE DEACON

Irish American News
WBEZ Public Radio
May 1999

I was once a pretty good altar boy. Not like the altar boys or girls you see at church these days. These kids barely know the moves.

They sit there on the altar with that dazed look on their faces as the priest stares at them and has to practically shout, "Bring me the book, nincompoop!"

They don't even try to fake it, like we did in the old days. And we had to memorize Latin for cripesakes.

Most of the Latin was drummed into our heads starting at the age of about five or six. But there were a couple of prayers that were real tongue twisters, like the "Suscipiat". I could never remember more than the first three words of that one. So I would just bow my head as if praying fervently and mumble the rest into my surplice. "Suscipiat Dei, omnipotentae, ad altare deum, shoelaces, sheepskin sandwiches vobiscum!"

And it worked. Nobody knew. Not even the priest, he was too busy inhaling the wine. Our gang of altar boys would get our crack at the wine later in the sacristy after mass. And when we served funerals, weddings, or baptisms, we could pick up some cash in tips.

It was a cool job in those days. You got to act like a bigshot up there on the altar, you got closer to God, free wine, and a couple of extra bucks every once in awhile at a baptism. That kind of activity had me interested in a vocation until I discovered girls.

That's why I was so pleasantly shocked a few weeks ago when I received a letter from my pastor, Father Paul, asking me if I was interested in becoming a Deacon of the Catholic Church. Wow! I guess you don't know me very well Father.

Now deacons have been part of the Roman Catholic tradition for centuries, but it's just within the last twenty years that we've been able to catch their act in contemporary Catholic rituals. They've certainly helped fill the void with our current shortage of priests. Deacons are sort of like reserve quarterbacks the coach sends in to eat the clock, but they aren't going to get you to the goal line. They can't celebrate mass, absolve you of your sins, or patch you through on that long distance call to the Big Guy in Heaven. But they do officiate at weddings, baptisms, and some of them get the opportunity to give sermons. This was the part that appealed to me, an opportunity to sling my malarkey from the pulpit on Sundays.

However those same people who would be sitting in the pews on Sundays listening to me rhapsodize about the wedding feast at Cana might be making jokes about my own futile attempts at turning water into wine at the local pub the night before.

In order for me to be a deacon I would have to be taken seriously, and that unfortunately is one sacrifice I'm not able to make. I have a few friends who are already deacons, and while their personalities are definitely not somber, they certainly wouldn't be the ones flipping you the bird on the Dan Ryan if you cut them off on the way home from church. But I would.

I just can't help being a high profile sinner. Would the lady I insulted after too many beers at the parish picnic flinch on Sunday when I offered her communion?

So I had my doubts about my success as a deacon. But my brother, who had spent some time in the seminary many years ago, told me, "I think deacons are supposed to get some kind of salary." All of a sudden I was interested again. The deaconate involved a three-year program of study at night and on weekends, which had initially scared me off, but if they were going to pay me to behave myself, perhaps I should investigate further. I decided to go to the introductory meeting the following week at the home of my friend John O'Neill, a deacon at our parish for over twenty years.

When I arrived there were about twenty people in attendance, mostly potential deacons and their wives. Everybody was very cordial and friendly, but one of the candidate's wives' jaw dropped when she saw me at the meeting, as if to say, "Who invited you?" Once again my reputation had preceded me. I suddenly felt like Larry Flynt at a nun's convention.

There were several deacons from our parish at the meeting and they gave us the low-down on the requirements and benefits of joining their tribe. I had already concluded that it was way out of my league when the question and answer session started.

I raised my hand and inquired as innocently as I could, "You know my wife told me not to ask this question, but I've got two kids in college, and I hate to sound like a Philistine, but can ya make any money at this?"

I don't think they took me seriously, because most of the group chuckled, aside from the fishwife who had earlier shot me daggers across the room. She fixed me with a scornful evil eye and glanced at her husband as if to say, "Satan is trying to infiltrate and you just sit there doing nothing?"

The deacon who was running the meeting laughed and replied to my question, "Well you don't make any money, but the insurance is great."

We repaired to our host's kitchen after the meeting for refreshments and I was privately lamenting my short lived career as a man of the cloth, when one of the deacons from our parish, Paul Faherty, took me aside and conspiratorially whispered in my ear, "Sometimes you can pick up a couple of extra bucks at a baptism.".

THE MONSTER

Irish American News
WBEZ Public Radio
June 1999

My wife has several pet names for me. "Monster" is probably her favorite. It's not meant as a term of affection, nor is it a testament to my larger than life personality.

"Monster" is usually hurled my way in the heat of battle while we are balancing the checkbook and I make the mistake of questioning some of her purchases. "I'm living with a monster!"

But last week we had another monster terrorizing our household. The lovely wife summoned me into the kitchen late Saturday night and instructed me to listen at the wall. There was something in there all right. I could hear it crawling, scratching, and growling its way across the soffit above the counter.

I knocked on the wall and it replied with an angry "Skreeeebl, skreeebl skreeeeeebl!"

It had somehow entered our duct system through a fan vent on our roof.

"It sounds like a bird. Forget about it. It will be dead in the morning."

But Mrs. Monster would have none of that.

"How do you know what it is? It could be an animal of some kind, it could gnaw its way right through the wall and attack us!"

I went back to lying on the couch and watching the life story of Jesse "The Body" Ventura, and tried to forget about the evil forces trying to burrow their way into my life. Our house is already an animal kingdom with teenage sons. Now I'm supposed to get all excited about the four-legged variety?

And then about two am I was awakened from a lovely dream of being stranded on a deserted island with Elizabeth Dole. We were discussing foreign policy as she fashioned a three-piece suit for me made from fig leaves.

"Wake up, wake up, that thing in the wall is driving me nuts."

It was the missus again, yanking me out of bed and towards the kitchen. She usually stays up much later than I and the intruder was making a heck of a racket, disturbing her nightly ritual of cataloguing my sins.

I buried my head in the pillow and told her there was nothing we could do at this hour as I tried to summon President Dole back into my dream to grant me the ambassadorship to Ireland.

"I'm calling the fire department!"

The fire department? Now I was awake and had visions of firemen over at my house in the middle of the night, looking tired and ticked off and shooting me glances of contempt for not being man enough to battle the monster myself.

"That's crazy. What's the fire department going to do? Where the hell is the fire?"

But she called them, at two am on a Saturday night. Maybe there wasn't a fire, but "That thing could gnaw through our wiring and start a fire couldn't it?"

And of course they told her, "It's probably a bird, it'll be dead in the morning, go to sleep."

My wife told me the fireman who answered the phone sounded sleepy and very annoyed too. He could have been our next Supreme Allied Commander if she hadn't awoken him from the very same Dole dream.

On Sunday morning my wife ran into one of the local cops in the White Hen and asked him what we should do to rid our happy home of the intruder and does the village do varmint removals?

"Lady, an animal in your house is a private matter."

She said she wasn't sure if he was referring to actual beasts or animal husbandry.

So we called the emergency wildlife control guys and the only one working on a Sunday had to come from way the hell out in Minooka. They captured the culprit, a baby raccoon that had fallen into our ventilation duct and was dangerously close to clawing into my breadbox.

They set a trap on the roof for the mother and caught her too. And it only cost me three hundred bucks.

The baby looked so innocent and scared and my wife was the picture of compassion as she asked one of the trappers what they would do with their new captives.

He gave her his best "Deliverance" style grin and told her they release all the raccoons in the wild. Yeah right, I thought, the wilds of Minooka.

I followed them out to their truck with the traps and the Minooka Mounties were smoking cigs in my driveway, wearing coonskin caps.

"These guys just caught dinner." I thought as I handed over my big fat check. I looked in the back of the truck and felt awful. There was the baby and the mother raccoon in a cage, glaring at me as the old jalopy belched it's way down the street.

And I could swear as they pulled into the distance, that I heard the mother raccoon shout back at me, "You are a monster!"

AHAB'S ASS

Irish American News
WBEZ Public Radio
July 1999

Call me Ishmael, but summer in Chicago reminds me each year of the adventures I had as a kid shootin' the ol' white whale in the brisk waters of Lake Michigan.

Maybe the custom of white whalin' didn't start with me but that's the way I remember it.

It was in seventh grade and the hot July sun was beating down on our gang sitting on my front porch as we chugged Kool-Aid and moaned about our ennui. Too old to chase lightning bugs and bored with the monotony of our frenzied water balloon wars we had recently pooled all our dough from cutting Dr. Fleming's huge lawn and took the bus to Chinatown to try and score some firecrackers.

We met an Oriental teenager with an Elvis hairdo promising cherry bombs and watched him take our dough up a stairway on Wentworth Avenue and disappear from our sight forever. Back in our hood now the guys were getting restless and irritable as they lagged pennies across my stoop and felt the sweat trickling through their baseball caps.

And then I remembered how easy it was to have fun. "Hey, let's go over to Rainbow Beach and shoot some white whales!"

I had been instructed in the ways of the white whale from a west side kid by the name of Mike Carroll when we met at Camp Tivoli in Cecil, Wisconsin in 1959. Tivoli was an all boys summer camp run by the Norbertine Fathers, a group of Catholic priests who spent their summers playing the part of Father Flanigan to a hundred or so Pee-Wees at this Chicago expatriates Boys Town.

Mike Carroll was typical of the urban kid who had been shipped off to Tivoli, all his brothers went there, as did all mine, sometimes two or three in attendance each summer. Kids with brothers were the gang bosses of summer camp. You had instant back up if somebody tried to short sheet your bed or shove a frog down your pants.

Tivoli spelled backwards was Camp "I lov it", and we did. Three months of swimming, fishing, horseback riding, canoe trips pretending to be commandos, sleeping out under the stars and hearing stories about the Shawano Lake monster. It roamed through Quicksand Creek, and so the story went, had eaten a couple of Tivoli campers back in the forties.

Early each morning revelry would sound and Father Joe would meet us at the flagpole on the green, smoking a Newport in his Tivoli t-shirt. After the pledge of Allegiance and the Our Father we scattered in different directions for a day of cool kid stuff.

Once a month the priests brought all the kids to Green Bay and gave each camper three bucks, a ton of cash in those days. We all bought hunting knives and played Mumbly Peg until somebody would eventually get stabbed. I won the boxing trophy at Tivoli in 1959 and my brother Tommy won the Drama Award. I can still kick his ass.

I learned many lessons at Tivoli that summer: how to spot poison ivy, how to bait a fishhook, how to swear like a Norbertine priest, how to blow smoke rings, and most importantly how to shoot the white whale.

It was really very easy. Mike Carroll had told me about as we tread water and watched the swimmers from the girls camp, which shared Shawano Lake. You simply pull your swimming trunks down to your ankles while submerged, and then perform a dorsal flip, as your bare butt crests the surface of the water.

It's sort of like mooning underwater. And the fact that the sun doesn't shine on that part of the body creates the illusion of a white whale. It works best when accompanied by raucous shouts of "Thar she blows!" and sophomoric laughter.

And so in seventh grade I introduced shootin' the white whale to the Southside of Chicago, or at least that's the way I remember it. It caught on fast I can tell you that. In those days it seemed to be the perfect icebreaker when swimming near a group of girls.

But sometimes it got out of hand. The fat guys did the best white whales of course, as their huge butts would breach the waters of Lake Michigan.

And one day the lifeguard at Rainbow Beach flipped out and frantically called the Coast Guard when he mistook Tiny Donovan's white whale for Moby Dick.

THE DARK AGES

Irish American News
WBEZ Public Radio
September 1999

I recently had the opportunity to meet a rectal surgeon. As I waited in the examining room I pondered what would drive a man to this profession.

I'm certain he didn't start out life intending to spend his most productive years inspecting keesters. Somewhere along the line in medical school he probably decided to specialize and discovered that there was gold in them thar hills. Or valleys, as the case may be.

I decided against asking the doctor how he got into this line of work as he entered, attached a clothespin to his nose, and introduced himself.

He looked normal enough, sort of a benign personality with a greyish pallor to his skin. The result, I'm sure, of spending so much time squinting into the place where the sun don't shine.

As we shook hands I was comforted by the fact that his fingers were so small. I explained my situation as delicately as possible and he smiled, instructed me to disrobe and lay on my side on the examining table. He told me he would be back in a jiffy, he just wanted to run down the hall for a minute to throw up.

As I lay on my side I studied the maps that decorated the walls of the room, full color illustrations of the anal canal that evoked the image of some sick valentine.

I've found that my indoor plumbing requires a lot more maintenance since I've hit middle age. When I was a youth I could churn out cement blocks, barbwire, and molten lava with no problem. But all of those years of white castles, booze, and jalapeno pizzas had taken their toll. The ol' canal just ain't what it used to be and I'd recently fallen victim to what my Dad used to call the "Irish disease", hemmies!

Since colon cancer is one of the three top killers of middle aged men I had decided to get an expert opinion and thought maybe the Army Corps of Engineers might have to be brought in to remedy the situation, just like they did many years ago when they reversed the flow of the Chicago river.

I lay on the table in trepidation of the surgeon's examination and bemoaned the fact that this was yet another one I hadn't studied for.

I became aware of the subtle, low-key music piped into the entire suite of offices to calm the nervous patient. I could just barely make out the dulcet tones of Shirley Bassey singing that classic James Bond movie theme from "Gold finger". How soothing. I tensed up again as the doc entered and put on his work gloves. "He's the man, the man with the Midas touch!"

Maybe it was the music but he suddenly looked suspiciously like the late German actor Gert Frobe who had starred as 007's nemesis in the flick. Dr. Frobe squirted some ointment onto his gloves and said, "OK, let's have a look." Yeah, I thought, enjoy the viewoooooooooo.

And then it was over. Or was it. He said, "I've got to get some light up there." and he walked over to a cabinet and pulled out an instrument the size of a javelin. He inserted two shotgun shells into the end of the contraption and told me to relax.

"What the hell is that thing?" I cried in terror and Dr. Frobe laughed cruelly and said, "It has many names Mister Bond, but I like to call it the 'Liber-ace'!"

After I dried my tears and put my clothes back on Doctor Frobe gave me his analysis. "Mister Bond, you are going to die, but not from hemmies!" Turns out I didn't need surgery, I didn't have cancer, and things were looking up. He told me my problem would soon disappear if I just followed his advice.

"What do you expect me to do Goldfinger?" I asked. He handed me his bill for ten thousand dollars and told me, "What do I expect you to do Mister Bond? Why eat more fiber of course!"

LIBERAL BREAD

Irish American News
WBEZ Public Radio
October 1999

My son was rummaging through the breadbox and whining the other day that we had no "white" bread. He told me he wanted to make a salami sand-wich on white bread. After warning him that salami on white bread was surely the choice of a Philistine and pointing out the fine selection of other breads available in our home, (rye and whole wheat), he bellowed in dis-gust, "I'm just sick of liberal bread!"

Liberal bread? I was unaware that our family choice of bread represented a political leaning, and shocked as well since my politics would best be embodied in a twelve pack of whatever beer was on sale at the Jewel that week.

I thought back to my own youth when white bread was in abundance in our kitchen during the fifties. The first sinister infiltration of wheat bread to our home was carried out under the guise of our Catholic faith. My mom coped with an intense religious addiction and had restricted her bread purchases to white and the occasional fling with a lusty rye. But when Monk's Bread made its' appearance on the grocery shelves of middle America she felt obligated to make her contribution.

All the kids in our family had sneered suspiciously at the brown bread that had integrated our breadbox. It looked strange to us and our palates were fearful of this monastic manna from the Babylon aisle of the IGA. It also had little specs of what appeared to be sawdust in its complexion, which only reinforced our xenophobia.

It wasn't until every slice of Wonder Bread in the house had been consumed that my brother Johnny had courageously ripped open the loaf of Monk's Bread one day and attacked it with a dull knife and a potent mobilization of peanut butter and jelly. He wolfed the commie sandwich down with three ravenous bites and then flooded his mouth with an antidote of cold, white milk.

The rest of us kids sat at the kitchen table mesmerized by his act of sedition and waited for him to turn into a werewolf and start quoting Karl Marx. But he smiled as the milk dribbled down his chin and he pronounced his chewy manifesto, "Hey, it's not bad!"

My brothers and I leapt to the breadbox and began assaulting the rest of the loaf with butter, mayonnaise, mustard, lettuce, tomato, and even some good ol' fashioned American bologna. And it was good, it actually tasted pretty good. It was different, certainly not wholesome but more sophisticated than what we had been weaned on and we instantly felt more intelligent as we ingested this alien staff of life.

It even passed the toast test as superlatives poured from our lips and we shouted out in our new command of the French language, "Viva Le Difference!" My brother Willy announced to all the boys, "If Monk's Bread is this good, just think how great Nun's Buns must be?"

We were raised as Democrats but during the sixties I started embracing the ideology of the ultra sesame Melba. I met a girl in college who actually baked bread and together we would listen to Bob Dylan and inhale pumpernickel.

She performed several exotic tricks for me like squeezing lemon onto her tuna fish salad sandwich, which was always swathed in two heaving slabs of whole wheat. She initiated me into my first artichoke and one night in a bread induced frenzy I had sliced and sampled a kiwi on little pieces of toast, with no crust!

Maybe I didn't march in Grant Park during the '68 Democratic Convention but I watched it on TV while ingesting a whole-wheat pizza.

I protested the Viet Nam war and sipped vichyssoise. Ah, the simple humanity of cold soup. As I moved on with my life I mocked my middle class white bread munching heritage and thumbed through treatises Julia Child had written about the left wing, of a chicken. I had become a card-carrying member of the whole-wheat wobblies. I would have no more nibbled on Wonder bread than vote for Nixon.

But then I got married and had kids. Cold soup lost its charisma as I veered to the right and returned to Mulligan Stew. Rice was no longer exotic, and what the hell was wrong with noodles anyway?

I bought a car, and then a house, and suddenly the militarism of a big juicy steak had replaced my pinko sympathies for yogurt. But always, always there was the whole wheat bread, the one last bastion of my lingering radical diet.

Liberal bread? Indeed, my son had enlightened me to a new way of thinking. I embraced him and said, "Oh my son, thank you, thank you for pointing out the error of my ways. Take the car and buy us six loaves of Wonder Bread and get back here and I'll make you a delicious raw meat sirloin on white bread."

"What the heck is that?" he wondered.

I smiled with inspiration and told him, "We'll call it a Pat Buchananburger!"

MICHAEL JORDAN

Irish American News
WBEZ Public Radio
November 1999

I was walking by Marshall Field's window the other day. They have a big window display for this new cologne, "Jordan". Some marketing genius thought everybody would want to smell like Michael Jordan. He's the greatest athlete of the century, but do folks really think smelling like a basketball player is gonna make them attractive? I think of Michael Jordan and I'm thinking poetry in motion, I'm thinking superstar, but I'm also thinking sweat.

And how much are they charging for this stuff? You want to smell like Michael Jordan? You'll save money just running around the block about fifty times before your date. Lucky for Michael he doesn't have to do that since he already smells like Michael Jordan. But what about the rest of us? What do we want to smell like?

I remember in eighth grade using a lot of "English Leather". In retrospect the idea of smelling like some poofy polo player's saddle doesn't sound like much of an aroma, but us kids used to practically swim in it. I was also very partial to "British Sterling" in high school. Why would an Irish kid be wearing so much limey sweet water? I thought the girls liked it. They would swoon in my arms as they inhaled my United Kingdom cologne and then I'd burp and they'd get a whiff of the corned beef and cabbage on my breath and really go wild.

I swore off cologne as I got older. I preferred "aftershave". Lots of my pals were using this stuff years before we actually had to shave but it sounded more macho. Cologne was for swishies with scarves around their necks and emery boards in their back pockets. It even sounded sissified. "Cologne"? Hey isn't that a city in France for cripes sakes? It may sound fancy calling it "eau de toilette", but it still means toilet water.

You're not supposed to drink the stuff either. One hungover morning in my twenties I lurched into the bathroom with a slaking thirst and inadvertently picked up the Old Spice Lime bottle and got a very valuable lesson in chemistry. My tongue is still mad at me for that stunt. I recall the taste being similar to gasoline with a citrus flavor, after it had been ignited.

These days there's a million different colognes on the market, most of them with some celebrity's name attached to it, whether it's Liz Taylor, Nelson Mandela, or Will Perdue. It's all marketing. When you get down to the real nitty gritty it's basically designed to cover the smell of your gritty with lots of nitty. But why is our "gritty" such a bad thing to smell?

Whenever I finish a workout I take off my sweat soaked shirt and inhale the aroma of my stench. It's exhilarating and revolting at the same time. I know it's going to make me gag, but I sniff it anyway because that odor is a testimonial to my torture. I've come by my stink the old fashioned way. I earned it. It makes you feel good to know that you've somehow wrung all that funk out of your body. If it smelled good you'd feel like you were losing something of value. It's reaffirming to let it go.

So maybe that's the key to the marketing of the "Jordan" cologne. You pour it all over your sweat clothes after a workout so the guys in the locker room will think you really put out 110% in the gym, when you were actually just leaning on the treadmill watching "Good Morning America". And you take your gym bag home and your family gets a whiff and says, "Wow, this stinks, you must feel great!"

I'm going to start wringing out my sweatshirts into a bottle and labeling it "Hooligan", the musk of the middle aged man. The label will tell you how it is developed from a fine blend of stale beer and liver sausage sandwiches.

I'll buy a factory in Berwyn and have hundreds of old Irish guys doing pushups all day as they lean over funnels and lift their pits for pennies. And then we'll send it over to London for their teenagers to try in revenge for all those years we were suckered into English Leather. We'll put it in a bottle shaped liked my head, bumps and all. All those Cockney punkers will soon be wearing the fragrance of a fifty-year-old frump.

I'm hoping to have it in stores this Christmas. You might even see it in the window of Marshall Fields as you walk by and say to yourself, "What a perfect gift for old Uncle Seamus, he smells like a billy goat on bath day now, maybe Hooligan is just what he needs!" Only $39.95 an ounce.

THE TRIBUNE BRIBE

Irish American News
WBEZ Public Radio
December 1999

I got a letter from the Chicago Tribune the other day. It was kind of inter-esting. The first part reads, " Dear Mr. Houlihan, We are in receipt of the t-shirt and bottle of Bushmills Irish Whiskey sent to our staff member Richard Christiansen on behalf of your company. All editorial employees are governed by an ethics policy that precludes them from accepting any gifts or promotional items. Therefore, we have donated the items to a char-itable organization."

Christiansen is the Tribune theatre critic. I had sent Mr. Christiansen this "gift" as a reminder on Sept. 17th that we were half way to St. Patrick's Day. I usually perform my show GOIN' EAST ON ASHLAND every year around Paddy's Day. So I like to grease the wheels a little bit, if you know what I mean.

Since Bushmills Irish Whiskey is one of the sponsors of my show they very kindly send me a case of the glorious stuff each year. So share the wealth is what I'm thinking and it wouldn't hurt to spread it around where it might do me some good. Christiansen has been pretty good to me in the past. In one review several years ago he said I was "terrific". And in his review of GOIN EAST ON ASHLAND, he said I was "a big, sandy-haired fella with a slight paunch and a natural storytellers flair." So thanks for that Richard, especially the "slight" description of my paunch.

So a guy like that you just naturally want to throw some love back in his direction. Hence the t-shirt from my show and the bottle of Bushmills. But please, mister Tribune executive who sent me the letter, I certainly would never consider my gift as a "bribe".

If I was gonna bribe the guy I would have sent over the whiskey wrapped in a couple of hundreds and delivered by a sexy blonde. Hey, I know how to make a drop for crying out loud. I learned from my dad first hand how you always offer to buy the policeman breakfast when he pulls you over for speeding.

So the fact that they mention the word "ethics" in my letter from the Trib doesn't bother me at all. I've got a clean conscience. Call it a professional courtesy, call it spreading some cheer on behalf of the Irish American community, call it a thoughtful reminder that St. Patrick's Day is only one hundred and eighty two and a half days away. But please don't call it a bribe. Give me more credit than that. I didn't just get off the Kedzie bus you know.

But what does cause me some concern in their letter is the fact that they have donated my t-shirt and whiskey to a "charitable organization". I just wish they could have told me which charitable organization.

If I see a homeless guy on lower Wacker Drive wearing a GOIN' EAST ON ASHLAND t-shirt sucking' on a bottle of Bushmills that's fine. If Monsignor McGillicuddy has whiskey on his breath and a bright green t-shirt under his vestments at midnight mass that's okay too.

But I certainly don't want some ACLU honcho staggering down Western Avenue at next years South Side Irish parade with my picture on his paunch. That could ruin my reputation.

I guess I should be thankful that Mr. Christiansen was honest enough to turn the booze and t-shirt over to his editors. If he didn't, he might feel he owes me and I certainly don't want that. I don't want him writing his next review with pangs of guilt over how easily he can be bought.

He might try and overcome those pangs with a very negative critique of the next Irish blowhard that comes along. And that might be me! No, I want him to write his next review of my show with a pure soul as he tells his readers of all the comfort and warmth I brought to the audience, not unlike a nice comfy t-shirt and the warmth of a couple shots of Old Bushmills.

So thanks to the Tribune for your letter and awakening me from my unethical stupor. I'll be watching the gutters and sacristies of Chicago for any signs of where my charitable donation winds up.

The only thing I'm alarmed about is that I never got any notes back from the Sun-Times. And I gave them two bottles of Bushmills.

CHAPTER FOUR
2000

MOM'S BOWL

Irish American News
WBEZ Public Radio
January 2000

I was watching the tube a few nights ago. I don't ordinarily watch television except for channel 11, Arts and Entertainment or the Howard Stern Show, but this night I was just surfing and got interested in a program which profiled the 100 most important people of the last millennium. It was heady stuff and covered characters like Sir Isaac Newton, Edison, Copernicus, and all the biggies. So it was down to the last three, building up to the most influential person of the last one thousand years.

I was watching with my sons and explaining who each significant person was as the program mentioned the contenders. They happened to be out of the room when the number one guy of the millennium was picked and came back when the show was over and asked me who it was. I told them "Guttenberg", and they agreed, "Oh yeah, Steve Guttenberg, he was pretty funny in those Police Academy movies."

I guess that was a lesson to me that everyone has their own perspective on time. As a guy who has lived for over half a century I like to think that my frame of reference is pretty all encompassing, but of course it isn't. You go to museums and you see artifacts of another era like Lincoln's knife and fork and you think, "Well big deal, it's just an old set of cutlery." But if you showed it to Lincoln he'd probably say, "Hey my old fork, the one Mary Todd Lincoln used to stab me in the butt with!"

Inanimate objects can somehow evoke a flood of memories of another time when we bump into them in the attic. They become totems to our own time, which would ordinarily just wind up in somebody else's garbage can. Let me give you an example.

My mom died about ten years ago and I was sent over to her apartment with my sister to clean out some of her stuff. After I had scoured the place in hopes that mom had stashed some rainy day cash somewhere I resigned myself to packing up the kitchen stuff.

Most of it was pretty new and held no particular significance. But then I found a red ceramic bowl way back in a cabinet that had sat in the kitchen throughout my youth. No, I didn't burst into tears thinking of all the hot oatmeal we had slurped from that bowl but I did grab it and hold it in my hands and suddenly felt transported to sixth grade.

If this bowl could talk I thought to myself. What would it say? "Sure I remember you. You always did a lousy job when it was your turn to wash me on Tuesdays, Thursdays, and Saturdays." This simple red bowl had not changed at all. It looked exactly the same. All the Irish stew, tuna fish salad, Easter egg coloring, and SOS pads had not marred her beauty.

I held her in my hands and marveled at the simplicity of her creation and subsequent existence. This uncomplicated red bowl had been witness to "the heartache and the thousand natural shocks that flesh is heir to". And yet she stoically stood the test of time, never changing, always comforting in her redness and white ceramic interior. I'm going to keep this bowl I thought, because she has no anxiety, no pretension, and holds no grudges. This bowl suckled our dreams, our hopes, and our future as a family. And unlike the rest of my family, the little red bowl was without a crack.

Since my sister had inherited all the furnishings my mom had left behind I surreptitiously slid the bowl under my jacket as we packed up the car. I was no longer upset at my mom for throwing out my high school football letter and 1959 boxing trophy from Camp Tivoli. They were mere knickknacks compared to her little red bowl.

I smiled as we drove and thought of how I would show my sons the bowl and tell them stories of the night my dog Muggs had leapt onto our kitchen table and wolfed down the French onion dip the bowl presented next to a box of Jay's potato chips. My sister and I had sat at the table that night munching and quizzing each other on the spelling of hors d'oeuvres that was written on the box. We had laughed uproariously as Muggs vomited the dip all over our kitchen floor. And I'm sure the bowl laughed too, in her own inscrutable way. Silently, bemused as she sat there in her ceramic redness.

I'm going to protect this bowl in my own kitchen for the next fifty years. And maybe someday I would wear it on my head for my grandchildren and make them laugh at grandpa's senility. Yes my little red bowl and I had plans.

I chuckled as I exited my sister's car and the little red bowl cascaded to the driveway and smashed into eight red ceramic pieces.

"What was that?" my sister said accusingly as I looked down at the pavement with tears in my eyes.

"Nothing. Nothing, just a bowl, a little red bowl."

NUDE THEATRE

Irish American News
WBEZ Public Radio
February 2000

I go to the theatre sporadically here in Chicago. I know I should go more often, particularly since I occasionally work in the theatre and have actually written a play or two. But I'm prevented from being a frequent playgoer because of my budget and my lazy butt.

However, the other night a kindly producer gave me some complimentary tickets and I figured I'd better check out the competition on Halsted Street. The show had been advertised as having adult content, nudity, and violence. So I was naturally looking forward to my night out.

After wrestling a small, stocky Hispanic fella for a parking space next door, my wife and I got into line for our tickets. I have a love-hate relationship with complimentary tickets, ("comps"), because I enjoy receiving them and absolutely detest giving them away. Certainly they are a necessary evil in the business. They help promote word of mouth about your show. But I also feel that if somebody wants to see my act for free, well hey, catch me in the bar, not after I've spent my kids entire college tuition fund advertising to get you to pay to see it.

We took our seats and skimmed our programs as we waited for the lights to descend. I used to love to read actors biographies before a show in hopes that I would recognize them from some of their previous work. But lately I've been annoyed over their use of the few words they've been given, to tell me about their cat, or the fact that they are a Sagittarius. If that is the most important thing they can tell me about their career I immediately think of Bette Davis in "All About Eve" when she announced, "fasten your seatbelts, it's going to be a bumpy ride!"

One of the actresses in this particular show thanked her mother for her unwavering support. She must be the nude one, I thought.

The play began with a flash of lightning and a man knocking on a door, which was eventually answered by a woman wearing a t-shirt, just a t-shirt. Interesting I thought, the playwright has made a choice to get right down to business, no beating around the bush. The dialogue that followed makes that remark seem downright Chekhovian.

The next two hours were replete with murder for hire, matricide, drugs, betrayal, adultery, and incest. It had all the ingredients for a suspenseful spellbinder, albeit a laughable one. It was riddled with good moments. While the play was not exactly designed with your blue haired matinee ladies in mind, I don't consider myself a prude and ordinarily might be amused by such shenanigans. But late in the play after some more gratuitous nudity, the villain forced himself on the leading lady with a drumstick from Colonel Sanders Kentucky Fried Chicken.

At this point in the evening I whispered to my wife that I heard they would soon be casting for understudies and perhaps she would be interested in auditioning. She was not amused.

After the obligatory Grand Guignol scene of blood lust the play ended and the thespians took their bows. I looked at the program again and was shocked to discover that they were all members of the union. I guess they needed professional actors to bare their genitalia and have sex with a chicken leg in public.

I thought of the sacrifices I've made over my years in the theatre and was embarrassed at how insignificant they now seemed compared to these troupers and their commitment to their art. I felt belittled, in more ways than one.

As we drove home, I hummed that tune from A CHORUS LINE, "What I Did For Love!" and discussed our evening of theatre with my wife. We happened to be driving down Lawrence Avenue and passed the Admiral Theatre, with its' marquee announcing, "Chicago's very own all live nude stage revue." I turned to the missus and said, "If they tried to do that drumstick routine there, the cops would shut them down." She agreed, "Well of course, that's not legitimate theatre, it's not art."

As I wondered why I've never been offered comps to the Admiral Theater, I told her "You're right honey, that's not art. But it would be if they used a live chicken!"

INFAMOUS IRISHMEN

Irish American News
WBEZ Public Radio
March 2000

We Irish have a reputation for our bravado, sense of humor, and gift of the gab, but in some circles we are also quite renown for our collection of rogues, scoundrels, and blackguards. Somewhere in the Irish character is the propensity for stepping over the line. When our natural inclination for individuality is unchecked it can result in behavior, which can best be described as uncivilized, albeit charming. The treachery of an Irish villain is almost always accompanied by one or more of our better traits, whether it's loyalty, wit, or love of mom.

I grew up with an Irish American lad on the Southside of Chicago who was infamous for his outrageous stunts as a carouser. Bill Gilhooley had started entertaining our gang in sixth grade with his unique abilities to burp, vomit, and flatulate on cue. In his early twenties he added chug-a-lugging quarts of booze to his repertoire. He developed these talents along with a sledge-hammer knockout punch to become one of the Southside's most infamous rascals. It was always fun to watch him throttle the other fella, as long as it wasn't you. He's much older now of course and has retired his wicked ways to a more sedentary lifestyle. I still hear from him every couple of years, the occasional Christmas card from Statesville penitentiary.

As St. Patrick's Day approaches I think of Gilhooley and his ilk with affection. It seems to me that our pride to be Irish this day each year should not exclude our nefarious brothers who went on in life to prove the nuns right. The statue of limitations has no doubt expired on their crimes so let's take a moment to salute a few of our own who have gone down in history as infamous Irishmen.

Now some would say we must discourage any salutation of these rule breakers. But these fellas who went astray are also exemplars of the unique character of the Irish. We can't all be priests and cops; some of us must follow our fate and be crooks. Yes we must celebrate our Irish talents as poets, artists, and saints. But without some recognition of these ruffians of repute we wouldn't be Irish, we'd be Swedish!

So here's a short line up of some of my favorites.

Terrible Tommy O'Connor

Late in September of 1921 an Irish fella by the name of Tommy O'Connor was sentenced in Chicago to "hang by the neck until dead" for the murder of police detective Sgt. Patrick J. O'Neill. His date with the gallows was set for December 8th, the feast of the Immaculate Conception. His legend grew while he was incarcerated and tabloids began referring to him as "Terrible Tommy O'Connor". And then on December 4, just four days before the hanging, Terrible Tommy and three other prisoners overpowered six guards in the old Cook County Jail and escaped over the wall. He's never been captured, although hundreds of sightings have been reported all over the country through the years. As you're looking over the marchers in this years' St. Patrick's Day parade keep an eye out for suspicious looking hundred-year-old men. The late Chicago Tribune reporter Tom Powers used to write a column back in the seventies each year on the anniversary of his escape. Powers opened with this plea, "Dear Terrible Tommy O'Connor, if you are still alive, please contact me so I can quit writing these columns, call collect!"

While Tommy may have sent some others to an early grave, legend has it that he was always deeply respectful and loving to his old mum. Supposedly he had once removed the thumb of a butcher who had overcharged Mrs. O'Connor on her rump roast.

Dion O'Bannion

On November 10, 1924, three years after Terrible Tommy O'Connor's escape, a dapper florist named Dion O'Bannion was gunned down in his shop just across the street from Holy Name Cathedral. Deanie had been an altar boy at Holy Name as a youth growing up in poverty with only his poor widowed plasterer father to watch over him. As a kid Deanie peddled papers on the Loop streetcars. His cherubic face belied his ability as a hoodlum and the lad was soon on his way as an Irish gangster. He got his first break as a terrorist during one of the newspaper circulation wars, and then graduated to bootlegging and killing with the Old Market Street gang. He became head of the North Side Combine and many said his florist shop was just a front for his wicked enterprises. But Deanie was a favorite of the widows who ordered flowers and his charm and constant courtesy went perfectly with his tailor made suits, which were specifically designed with pockets to carry his three revolvers. He could shoot with either hand and was known as a deadeye when he dispatched two men in the entrance to the LaSalle Theatre. Bad actors no doubt.

O'Bannion was known for his loyalty, a marvelous Irish trait. When one of his pals, Nails Morton, was killed by a horse that threw him, Deanie and his boys tracked down the horse, kidnapped it and led it back to the scene of Nails demise, and filled it full of lead.

Mickey Finn

We have to go back do the days soon after the Chicago Fire to find my favorite Irish blackguard. He was an ex-pickpocket who owned the Lone Star and Palm Garden Saloon at the end of Whiskey Row. His name was Mickey Finn and he served booze and B-girls to his clientele of Chicago desperadoes. Mickey was an enterprising guy who was always on the lookout for unique promotions to draw in the gullible greenhorns who made the mistake of waltzing through his door while slumming. He invented a drink, which he dubbed "the Mickey Finn Special", a combination of raw alcohol, water in which snuff had been soaked, and a mysterious white powder Finn claimed he had obtained from a Voodoo Doctor. The unfortunate traveler who quaffed a Mickey Finn Special would soon be goin' east on Ashland, rendered unconscious for the next two to three days. Our man Mickey would then rifle their pockets at his leisure, stripping the sucker of his clothes and dumping him in the alley. Upon awakening they never remembered a thing.

In true Chicago fashion Mickey Finn paid off the cops until one of the poor saps croaked and folks started asking questions. Mickey's joint was closed down in 1903, but his legend and the miraculous powers of the Mickey Finn Special live on today in Chicago, New Orleans, Shanghai, and sleazier saloons all over the world. Mickey may have been a murderer, but in the best tradition of Irish barkeeps, every fourth drink was a buyback. If you made it that far!

The spirit of Mickey Finn lives on as well in a thousand different spots in our city. Their carrying the flag for the dark side of Chicago's Irish today, the scoundrels and rascals who give us all a bad name. But without them the Irish would just be a group of Kellys, Murphys, and Daleys. While guys like Terrible Tommy O'Connor, Deanie O'Bannion, and Mickey Finn have paved the way for the Hooligans in our midst!

SORRY FOR YOUR TROUBLES

Irish American News
WBEZ Public Radio
April 2000

Like any good Irishmen I read the obituary column every day. It's a habit I picked up from my Dad. He used to read the Tribune, Chicago American, and the Daily News every day just for the obituary columns. He'd be sittin' at the kitchen table scanning the columns of the deceased and he'd say to me, "Time to review the Irish scratch sheet. I'm just checkin' to see if I croaked!"

Some folks may think this a bit macabre, but we Irish are always on the lookout for a good wake. And we read the entire obit box with the names of all the descendants and relatives, just in case Mr. Larry Zawacki had married into the Murphy family, who of course we all knew from St. Cajetans parish.

Obit scanning can help when you are visiting a funeral home for the wake of Tommy O'Reardon, and the next parlor is hosting the Zawacki mourners. Then you can kill two birds with one stone and drop by to see the Murphy in-laws and tell them "sorry for your troubles."

I've met guys in bars who bragged of hitting three wakes in one night at the same funeral parlor. We call that a "triple double!"

Last week I was perusing the death notices and I recognized a guy with his picture in the obit box. That's the latest thing I guess. The Sun-Times has been pitching it a lot, for a more personalized death notice. So I see this guy's photo, Chicago paramedic Mike Smith, looks like he was fine broth of a man, a retired firemen. And I thought to myself, "Mike Smith? Seems to me he died a couple times in the last month. Yeah, as a matter of fact I've read this guys obit about ten times. When the hell are they going to bury this guy?"

Well it turns out that it was actually an ad the Sun-Times is using to demonstrate how great your personalized death notice would look. And they just keep using poor ol' Mike Smith's photo and fake story. Geesh, I was ready to go out and buy his family a shovel and tell them to get busy.

I was telling my ol' buddy Skinny Scanlan about this and he told me a story of the Monahan family who visited their father Monk's grave several times each year for over ten years. Then they get a letter from the cemetery informing them that they have discovered that Monk Monahon isn't buried there. They made a mistake and Monk is actually buried in Alice Blomquist's grave about a football field away on the other side of the graveyard.

And for the last ten years the Monahans have been getting down on their knees in the rain, hot sun, and especially on Monk's birthday in December and offering up their prayers for Monk's eternal salvation. Monk's son Jerry was particularly peeved, "All those years I been saying rosaries for Alice Blomquist, some old bag I never laid eyes on!"

I'm sure Miss Blomquist was happy to send those prayers in the direction of Monk but not without taking some kind of prayer commission. For the last ten years she's probably been cutting a decade or two out of each of those rosaries the Monahans were saying and lemme tell ya, that adds up. So you can understand how the Monahans felt a bit swindled. Alice Blomquist might be in Heaven now merely because she was in the right place at the right time.

I usually try to stop by and visit my Dad's grave every year around St. Patrick's Day. Dad never really made that big a deal about that grand Irish feast day, but it just so happens that he's buried in Holy Sepulchre Cemetery. That's right around the corner from Reilly's Daughter saloon, where I make an annual St. Patrick's Day pilgrimage. So I always stop to shoot the breeze with my late Dad.

He's buried in our family plot, which is just a football field away on the other side of graveyard from the late, great Mayor Richard J. Daley's final resting place. Hmmmmm, I wonder if those same wise guy gravediggers who planted Monk Monahan might have slipped my pop into the Mayors spot? Actually that's ok with me because I'm a sure "da mare" get tons of prayers said for him out at Holy Sepulchre. Take the commission Pop, that kind of clout has gotta be worth a plenary indulgence at least.

CRITIQUING THE CRITICS

Irish American News
May 2000

"The theatre is a cruel mistress." I don't know who said it but he couldn't have spent more dough on that bitch than I have. For twenty-seven very odd years, I have been chasing that theatrical slut like a drunken sailor with a fist full of fifties. I've had some wild times with this enticing trollop, but mostly she has lured me in with her seductive promise of passion only to smack me in the kisser when she unleashes her hounds of hell, the critics.

It's a common belief in show business that if you are stupid enough to believe the critics when they praise you, it will only be a matter of time before they turn on you and march you to the guillotine. I choose to believe that the ones who praise me are obviously geniuses and when they eventually attack it's because they must have gone off their medication and need to destroy what is truly beautiful to them. It's the old Irish custom of chopping off the head of the first person that tries to lift his head above the crowd to look around. "It's the horse with the dirtiest arse which lifts its tail so high!"

But do we ever give up? Never. After opening my latest theatrical production last week and taking my kudos and kicks, I'm ready to give a sanguinary salute to the critics of Chicago. Yes, I have pity on these parasites as they feed off our endeavors. I'm perfectly willing to acknowledge the brilliance of the few, particularly the critics of the Chicago Tribune and Daily Southtown. Those two are obviously very gifted and insightful evaluators of the theatrical art. But some of their brethren in the biz are now subject to my acute astuteness.

On opening night I stood at the stage door just a half hour before the curtain went up having a smoke and shooting the breeze with the director of my play.

"What are you gonna do with YOUR money?"

As we chuckled over this absurdity, we were approached by a disheveled lard of a man in a stained trench coat that hadn't been washed since the Bijou Theatre closed down years ago during the Gerry Ford administration. His distinct odor announced his presence and I turned to see him smiling at us through his immense beard, still mottled with the ketchup he had consumed with his frankfurter at the Andy Warhol Film Festival of 1986. I was about to tell him he was too late for the auditions of One Flew Over the Cuckoo's Nest across the street, when he clutched his plastic-bag-wrapped notebook to his bosom and introduced himself as the critic for the Chicago Reader.

As I read his brief but scathing review a week later, I hoped they were paying him by the word. I should have known he would hate the play; anyone who puts ketchup on a hot dog is obviously nuts!

We also received a bile spewing bashing from a fella named Winters writing for a paper I was heretofore unfamiliar with, New City. Mr. Winter's discontent was aimed directly at our cast, exhausting his Thesaurus and labeling us all with a two-syllable vulgarity used to describe the exit of the alimentary canal. I was shocked and amused by the depth of his vocabulary and thought what a New City it is indeed when their writers creative juices are wiped across the pages of their paper.

Interesting that both these "newspapers" are free of charge to the public. They obviously make so much money from all the prostitutes advertising in the paper they can afford to give it away.

But throw them away folks; because their opinions are like that two-sylla-ble vulgarity, everybody's got one. They certainly couldn't match the out-rage of one lady who sent me a letter demanding her money back after seeing my play. "If I wanted to be subjected to that, I would rent a porno video and/or go to a bar!"

Of course I couldn't refund her money because she just might spend it on one or the other of those two very unwholesome pursuits. Perhaps she could look into a career as a drama critic with the Reader or New City, where one of the perks most certainly would be complimentary tickets to bars that screen porno videos.

As long as we still have geniuses writing for the Tribune and Daily South-town, the theatre will survive. Their rave reviews and keen insight into the comedy and style of my new play are the aphrodisiac, which keeps me knocking on that mistress' door. I was also blessed to receive a very nice review from the newspaper Outlines, which is the weekly voice of the Gay, Lesbian, Bi & Trans community of Chicago. And my gratitude for that can only be expressed in the words of the late band leader Lawrence Welk, "Dank you boys!"

BEDWETTER

Irish American News
WBEZ Public Radio
August 2000

I was driving by the local schoolyard the other morning and saw a bus parked and waiting for the kids as their parents sent them off to summer camp. It brought back some great memories of my days as a kid at summer camp.

All five of my older brothers had attended Camp Tivoli in Cecil, Wiscon-sin. When I reached the age of nine it was my turn to spend July and August in the care of the Norbertine Fathers as they taught us horseback riding, swimming, boating, archery, boxing, and the fine art of mumbly peg.

The camp was all boys and they ranged in age from ten to thirteen. I was allowed early admission to the camp only because of the long history of Houlihans who had been enrolled over the years. We lived in cabins, a dozen kids to a cabin, with a live-in counselor who bunked in front. The counselors were usually college guys who had taken the summer job of supervising a bunch of tyro Bowery Boys from the city. The priests lived in a bigger cabin on the other side of the baseball diamond. They said mass each day and were the gang bosses of the joint.

Cabin number one housed the oldest boys and each of the other seven cabins were home to lads of approximately the same age. The youngest guys were all in Cabin Eight and Cabin Nine was the showers and toilets. That was one of the big jokes, "Hey, I gotta visit Cabin Nine!"

I spent four summers at Camp Tivoli and had a blast. But that first season was not without it's trauma for this tyke away from home for the very first time. My folks had sent along my older brother Tommy for his last summer and they figured he'd keep an eye on me if I got homesick or scared. But Tommy was housed in Cabin One with the big guys and that chasm between his bunk and mine in Cabin Eight seemed impenetrable. The only time I ever saw him was each morning as we all washed up together in Cabin Nine and there he would greet me with a wedgie or noogie to let me know he cared.

My counselor was a seminarian named Dick Brophy who was still under the illusion that life was all on the square. He startled me awake one night with a flashlight in my face as he announced to the world, "Mike, you've peed in your bed!" I'd been a sporadic bed wetter for years up to that point and never thought it was that big a deal. Besides, cabin nine was a good hundred yards away in the woods and I wasn't about to venture out there in the dark night. I had heard too many stories from my brothers of Tivoli campers who had been swallowed up by the monster of Quick Sand Creek on their way to nocturnal relief.

But Brophy complained of the odor from my bed and decided he was going to break me of the habit. He guided me with the flashlight and instructed me to take a leak off the front steps of the cabin. Then he pulled a towel from my locker and told me I must wear it as a diaper until my bedwetting ceased. I went back to my bunk humiliated and dreamed of the day my four older brothers would come to pick me up and play kickball with Brophy's head.

Of course the news was out the next morning as the entire camp assembled at Cabin Nine before mass. I was washing my face when I heard the shrieks of Davey Dooley, the kid who bunked above me. "Houlihan peed in his bed! Houlihan peed in his bed!" Everybody laughed and asked me how I liked my diaper. I turned to my brother Tommy with stinging eyes and he chortled and said, "Mike, you peed in your bed? That's goofy." I was backed up against the urinals and flung my wash cloth in Davey Dooley's face and challenged him to a boxing match that Saturday night.

I didn't win that fight. It was a draw. But I did go on to become the 1959 boxing champion of Camp Tivoli. Later in the summer someone stole some money from Dick Brophy's locker. Of course I was fingered as the first suspect. The other counselors brought me in and "asked my help" in finding the culprit. "Just because I wet the bed, that don't make me a thief!" Another kid eventually confessed to the crime and I was given new respect.

I wondered how many bed wetters were getting on that bus for camp as I drove by the schoolyard the other morning. I prayed that none of them would run into a counselor like that dork Dick Brophy. I wonder if he ever became a priest. Maybe he's working a parish in Chicago right now, dispensing his wisdom. He was so naive to think I would try to get back at him by stealing his money. I would never do anything as small-time as that for revenge. No, it would be something much more public, something more humiliating. Something like this.

PAROCHIAL POLITICS

WBEZ Public Radio
November 2000

Someone once remarked on the rough and tumble world of politics that "It ain't beanbag!", and how right they were.

Recent snafus in the national election reminded me of a very dirty presidential campaign I was involved with in 1994. My son Paddy was running for President of his eighth grade class at St. Luke elementary school. The presidency was usually bestowed upon the smartest kid in class, a nice lad named Bazook Patel. But Paddy had decided to challenge Bazook for the simple reason that he thought he could get more votes. He mistakenly thought that since he had played a lot of sports and had a winning personality that he might have a shot. After all, Bazook had spent most of his time in the last eight years sucking up to the teachers, getting straight A's, and winning the state science fair with his human heart transplant experiment.

Paddy's opponent had racked up quite a few accomplishments but my son reminded me that he was no slouch at the science fair either. His experiment involved the effects of dog doo on the typical lawn and was lauded by his classmates as outstanding and by his teachers as one that definitely ranked.

Bazook's father had designed some nifty laminated buttons and signs for his son's campaign. Even though I had some experience working on campaigns in Chicago politics I bit my tongue and decided not to interfere, unless I was called upon for some last minute dirty tricks.

So I was honored when my son asked me if he could read me his speech the night before the election. Paddy would be delivering his speech the next day before the entire school at assembly and he was admittedly a bit nervous. He launched into his speech with a laundry list of his accomplishments over the years at St. Luke and his vision for the future of their eighth grade class. When he finished he looked at me with anticipation and said, "So, what do you think Dad?"

"It's good. But where's the jokes?"

I then explained to him how important a bit of levity in the speech would be to humanize him and help his image as a man of the people. He looked at me quizzically, "Jokes? About what?"

"Well, you should try and find a joke that all the kids can identify with, maybe a joke about something or somebody that the whole school can relate to. Who's the biggest dork in the school?"

His brother Bill, who had been sitting on the couch with me listening to the speech, chimed in, "Yeah, what about that yutz, Mr. Gideon?"

They both started laughing and explained to me that Mr. Gideon was a teacher's assistant, who weighed about four hundred pounds, with black, horn rimmed, coke bottle glasses, wore his pants around his nipples, and was constantly breathing his horrific breath all over the students in study hall. They assured me that Mr. Gideon was known by every kid in the school and was probably the biggest geek that ever walked the earth, let alone the halls of St. Luke.

I beamed at their political acumen and told them, "Sounds to me like Mr. Gideon is your man. Now write a joke about him and you can start planning your inaugural."

The next day Paddy called me at work from the principal's office. "Thanks a lot Dad."

"Paddy, did you win?"

"No I did not win, and I think I'm about to be expelled from school."

The principal then got on the phone and informed me that she would like to meet with me the next day at school with several of the teachers and the pastor. That night I got the full story from the boys as my wife, the pundit, offered her critique of the campaign. "You idiot, what possessed you to tell him to do that?"

They told me how Paddy and Bazook had stood on the stage in front of the entire school and delivered their speeches. Bazook had gone first and had the girls and all the teachers practically weeping with his eloquence. And then Paddy had delivered his speech, and at the very end proclaimed, "And if I am elected as President of the St. Luke eighth grade class, there will be no more Mr. Gideon's in this school!"

Evidently this final witty remark had triggered pandemonium with students laughing and cheering and chanting "Paddy for President!" This was imme-diately followed by the principal grabbing the microphone and admonish-ing the electorate as Paddy was dragged from the stage by Mrs. Mogen, the very large eighth grade homeroom teacher and a secret admirer of Mr. Gideon.

At the meeting the next day I was lectured by Mrs. Mogen screaming in my ear about "respect". I barked right back at this harridan that "Respect must be earned, and if you're thinking about kicking my kid out of school for making a joke, then perhaps I should go to the school board and discuss how you "fixed" the election by telling all the kids not to vote for anyone who had made an improper remark."

This act of brinkmanship resulted in a happy compromise. Paddy would return to school and there would be no demand for a recount. On graduation day Paddy gave me a note thanking me for my support in the election aftermath. When I asked him if he had given up on politics forever after the Mr. Gideon fiasco, he told him he would have to think about it. But he also said he had learned something from the experience.

"Politics. It ain't beanbag, Dad."

JACKIE CASTO'S CHRISTMAS STORY

WBEZ Public Radio
The Beverly Review
December 2000

I stopped into Ken's the other night, my favorite south side watering hole. My old pal Jackie Casto was behind the bar, the best bartender in the City of Chicago. There is no prescribed "buy-back" policy at Ken's like some joints where every fourth drink is a buy-back. But when Casto is behind the bar you can walk in the door and throw a sawbuck on the mahogany and walk out with thirteen bucks. It's just a cozy joint with great regulars where the beer is always cold and on top of that they make a kick-ass Manhattan.

You can really sink a root at Ken's and it makes it hard to leave. Some folks have said that it's easier to get out of Cook County Jail than it is to leave Ken's when Casto is in a good mood.

And Jackie was in a very good mood the other night, full of Christmas cheer. I was actually taken aback at his holiday enthusiasm because he can sometimes be cranky. Victims of his fervent cynicism may describe him as a grinch but when Jackie is under doctor's orders to curb his appetites he's more like the grinch's junkyard dog. But this night Jackie was practically ho-ho-hoing across the bar as he greeted me, "Houli-Houli-Hey Merry Christmas Houli."

In light of Casto's Yuletide cheer I decided to go with the hard stuff, and ordered a Mannie. Jackie flipped a coaster under my canarb, lit up a smoke and leaned across the bar.

"Houli, you will never believe the night we had in this joint last week."

As a witness to many debauched nights in that joint I was ready to believe anything. I had seen things happen in Ken's that ordinary mortals merely have nightmares about. I once saw a woman take a running start and leap over the bar in a single bound on a fifty buck bet. But that's another story. This one, Jackie Casto's Christmas story, has a happy ending.

Jackie beamed at me. "I was working the bar the night of the Three Kings Concert and this guy walks in the door with a young girl, pregnant, couldn't have been more than sixteen. She sits at a booth and the guy comes up and asks me for a glass of water."

I stopped Jackie then and asked him what was the Three Kings Concert. He explained that it was an annual Christmas concert at the Beverly Art Center with three Elvis impersonators doing carols. "It's kind of like the three tenors only a whole lot funkier."

I gazed up at the wall and there was the poster, Live at the Beverly Art Center, One Night Only, The Three Kings-Elvis Gamboni, Elvis Murphy, and Elvis Washington. Command Performance of the south side's three greatest Elvis "interpreters".

Jackie grabbed my arm as he has a tendency to do when he is making a point or screaming in your ear about the point spread, "So the place is packed with people coming in after the show, and this guy walks in with the knocked-up kid and asks me for a glass of water for his wife. So right away I knew something was kinky cause this kid in the booth looked more like she could be his daughter. I give him the water and he tells me his car threw a rod on Western and he was tryin' to take his wife to the hospital because she's about to give birth. I'm grabbin' for the phone to call 911 and the next thing I know this girl lets out a screech and Frankie Moran sitting at the bar says 'Too late for that Jackie, looks like it's coming now.'

So the place goes nuts as Mary Jo and the waitresses jump into action. Fred O'Riley and his wife are havin' dinner here and she's a nurse at Little Company, and Frankie Mo has made tons of paramedic runs as a fireman, and the place is loaded with off-duty cops anyway, and Cathy Clancy brings out a bunch of tablecloths and the next thing you know booth number three is a delivery room. And Jimmie Goff is sittin' at the end of the bar shouting at me, "Boil some water!"

So this guy Joe is right in there and sayin' "Push Mary, Push, and then everybody in the joint is sayin' it, "Push Mary Push." And out pops the kid, a boy. I cut the umbilical cord with this lime knife. So the girls clean the kid off and wrap him up in some napkins, the nice ones. And Frankie checks the kid's vital signs, checks the mother too and says everybody is ok. I got every customer in the joint hovering over booth number three and they're all oohing and ahhing and Goff took up a collection for the kid right there and raised eighteen hundred bucks.

So I buy a round for the house in honor of the kid and his mom and who walks in the door but the Three Kings. I forgot that I had promised Tuna Carey a yard and a half if he could get them to come in my joint for a drink after the show. I don't know how he did it, but there they were, in their outfits too. And Frankie takes one look at them and says, "I'm glad you guys are here because I have tidings of great joy!"

And Goff hits them up for the collection and they start telling us that Elvis never carried cash. But Elvis Gamboni gave him one of his gold chains, and Elvis Murphy came up with a decanter of Michael Jordan cologne he had out in the car, and Elvis Washington kicks in his stash of primo Sensimilla. And then Washington breaks into the sweetest rendition of "Silent Night" I ever heard. We're all standing there and you could hear a pin drop and I swear the spirit of Elvis came upon him as he crooned, "sleep in heavenly peace."

And I looked over at this young girl holding her baby in the booth and he's asleep, and at the end of the bar Goff had fallen asleep too. With this peaceful little smile on his face.

I was on my third Manhattan by now and Jackie's story had amazed me.

"That's incredible Jack, a guy named Joe and his wife Mary gives birth to a baby boy in your bar, and then is visited by the Three Kings, do you realize the significance of this? All you needed was an ox and a lamb."

And Jackie says, "Oh we had that, I gave them some ox tail soup."

"What did they name the kid?"

Casto cackled as he freshened my drink, "What did they name him? Well what the hell do you think they named him?"

"You mean..?"

"That's right. They named him after me, Jackie. Merry Christmas Houli, the drinks are on me."

CHAPTER FIVE

2001

JOHN WALTERS

Irish American News
February 2001

"Mike, can you come over right away, old John has died and we need you to identify the body."

It was Bruno, the guy who lived across from me on the other side of 43rd Street in New York City.

"Old John" was John Walters, the dishwasher at O'Donnell's bar where I was employed in 1982 as the porter. John and I had become pals over the course of that very strange year. I didn't even realize he lived across the street from me until I happened to run into him one night in another bar, the Blarney Rock, a couple months after I had started at O'Donnells. He was probably around seventy, a skinny, short guy with huge ears, which was kind of ironic because he was stone deaf. You wouldn't think we had that much in common but John liked to drink and so did I.

I grabbed my coat and headed toward the elevator thinking back to the first day I met John. Pat Dooley was my boss at O'Donnells and he handed me the keys and told me to be there the next morning at 5:30 AM, to sweep and mop the floor, take the beer deliveries down the basement, and load all the coolers. I would work six days a week until around 9:30 in the morning, go home, shower and shave, and head off to my office on Broadway where I was pretending to be a hotshot producer.

Pat told me, "Old John will show up around 6:30, he'll get the kitchen ready for lunch, maybe he'll give ya some coffee, some breakfast. Ya get 75 bucks a week, cash. Make sure ya wash out the toilets and the urinals in the mens crapper, every day." I did the womens too, but compared to the mens it was Elysium.

The guy who had the job before me had left to go to college, he was eighteen. I was thirty-three, married with two kids, and living at 43rd and Ninth Avenue in section 8 housing for actors, dancers, and other showbiz wannabees. I found the job somewhat romantic in spite of my trepidation about scrubbing the urinals. There was something mysterious about O'Donnells. It had been in that location for something like 80 years and was a beer soaked old gin mill that stagehands, doormen, transit workers and cops hung out in. I hung out there too sometimes. That's how I got the job.

The only way you could communicate with Old John was with a half-assed form of sign language, writing it down, or getting up close and screaming directly into his ear. One morning I noticed the radio was gone from behind the bar and after gesticulating an elaborate pantomime accompanied by me shouting at the top of my voice, "What happened to the radio?", John said to me "There's instant coffee in the kitchen Mike."

Hell, he didn't miss the radio. So I gave up on my favorite program "The Milkman's Matinee" and started listening to John instead. And for the next couple hundred mornings and scores of visits at the Blarney Rock he told me plenty. It was a sad story but he didn't seem bothered by it. He had kids somewhere, in Philly I think. He was estranged from them. Booze does that. He'd gone deaf after getting rolled down on the Bowery years ago and now he lived in Bruno's boarding house, three squares a day, steady work and nobody bothered him.

I had visited his room once before when Pat Dooley sent me looking for him. He was laying in bed in his long underwear and smoking a Lucky and a nun from Holy Cross parish was there telling him he had to eat more regularly and to knock off the booze and cigs. I gave him a scarf for Christmas and the next day he was up and back at O'Donnells at the crack of dawn.

That was about three months before Bruno's call that morning. He buzzed me in and I walked up the stairs to John's room. Two uniformed cops were going through his belongings. "You know this guy?" I looked over at John on the bed, still wearing the longies and this look of pure shock on his frozen face.

His eyes were wide open and so was his mouth, in a tortured look of disbelief. There was a dried web of saliva strung across his toothless chasm and he looked like he had just laid eyes on something horrifying. I looked at the cop who was opening a tin band-aid box John had filled with quarters. His partner was hunting through the drawers and I said, "Did you find anything?" The cop with the quarters said, "Your gonna have to come down to the morgue later today and ID him again."

John had that same creepy look on his face at the morgue as his body was dumb-waitered up on a gurney and Bruno's pal the undertaker pulled the blinds up on the viewing window. The undertaker was a nice guy in a Herman Munster sort of way and he said, "Sign this Mike and I can claim his body and take it back to the funeral parlor." I looked at John, his eyes a frightened puppy, the spider web of spit was still there too. "Do me a favor," I said, "wipe that smile off his face for the wake."

The wake was just a couple blocks away on 39th Street, a funeral parlor that every bus leaving Port Authority cruised by a hundred times a day. Bruno said, "If you're not dead by the time you get here, the exhaust fumes from the busses will cinch it for you."

Mr. Munster came over and shook my hand and introduced me to the other three revelers at the wake, Bruno's daughter, the nun, and Mrs. Munster. Herman led me over to the casket and John was laid out in a grey, double-breasted suit with a big blotchy stain over the right pocket.

"Nice suit," I said.

Herman gave me a look, "Thanks, I picked it up on Ninth Avenue for eleven bucks. Oleg Cassini."

I knelt down and he faded into the back, "Of course." I made the sign of the cross and looked at Old John. He looked dignified. Alec Guinness on a bad day. On his worst day. Mr. Munster had taken away that mask of terror and replaced it with, if not serenity, at least begrudged acceptance.

I said, "John... you are dead. Get used to it old pal. I had a feeling all the time that you heard every word I said. So, listen to this John. When you get where you're going, put in a good word for me, and have that coffee, that breakfast waitin'. Amen."

THE LADS

Irish American News
April 2001

Many, many years ago on my 21st birthday, my mom surprised me with a magnum of champagne. My buddy Waldo was picking me up that night and we drank the bubbly out of juice glasses in the kitchen with my mom. Today both of them are in a state of bliss. My mom is in heaven and Waldo fell victim to an alcoholic brain disorder and is now in a nursing home in Waukegan, which he thinks is in Kansas.

I'm sure that birthday bottle had nothing to do with either of their present circumstances. But it did come to mind recently when my sons turned 21 and I cautioned them to "go easy". Just because you are legally allowed to imbibe when you hit that milestone doesn't mean you are required to go nuts. Don't use up all your coupons in one night. It took Waldo another 30 years of boozing before his brain blipped out.

Fortunately my sons behaved themselves on their 21st birthday. I don't mean they didn't flex their muscles as men that night. But they didn't get thrown in jail, drive or crack up the car, or even wind up driving the porcelain bus. They wouldn't have been allowed to operate any heavy machinery that night, but they were good.

The lads were born on March 15th. Shakespeare buffs will remember the words of the Soothsayer in JULIUS CAESAR when he approached Jules and told him, "Beware the Ides of March." And sure enough that was when Brutus and his boys backstabbed the boss. But for me it's always been a happy occasion to celebrate the birth of my boys and also the upcoming feast of St. Patrick.

I remember the day they were born in New York City. I was out late the night before till the wee hours. I had produced a show at St. Malachy's on 49th Street and we partied at a little joint across the street called The Tin Pan Alley. I made the mistake of hanging my coat on one of their wall hooks and somebody puked on it on their way out the door.

By the time I got home Mary was in labor. I lay on the bed next to her and she told me to time her contractions. At first they were coming slowly because I fell asleep between each one. But pretty soon she was smacking me every twenty minutes and we decided to make a run for the hospital.

A guy by the name of Jharlid Ishkabibble loaned me his watch to time the contractions while he taxied us to Lenox Hill Hospital. "If it's a boy, I won't be naming him after you." He wished us good luck as we hustled into the emergency room and the nurses took one look at Mary, plopped her into a wheel chair to a labor room and said, "Looks like the twins are on their way."

Mary lay in agony for the next five hours cussing me out and I kept telling her how beautiful she was and saying "breathe". Another nurse came in and asked if she had thrown up. "No, that's just my coat."

Dr. D. arrived and we wheeled the lovely Mary into the delivery room. She was hangin' tough goin' natural all the way. Billy popped out first and when Paddy tried to land feet first after him, the Doc reached inside and performed a dipsy doodle to the astonishment of the assembled group. Paddy finally appeared head first nine minutes later like the Fridge squeezing across the goal line.

We were blessed with two healthy boys and I went downstairs and bought them a Nerf football in the gift shop. I'll never forget the look on Mary's face afterwards, like that little girl they rescued from the mineshaft.

On the way home I grabbed a cab on Fifth Avenue. The street was being prepared for the St. Patrick's Day parade and it was a beautiful sunny day. I told the cabbie, "I just had twin sons! I feel like I won a million dollars." And he said, "You'll need it — they will wind up costing you a lot more than that!"

Twenty-one years later I have to admit he was right. If I had a nickel for every nickel I've forked over for braces, Buicks, and bail money I'd be loaded. Of course it was all worth it. Trump couldn't buy the happiness these guys have given me.

On their birthday last month I was once again doing a show and worked late into the night. Paddy was partying downtown but I caught up with Bill in Doc Ryan's just a few minutes before closing. I put my arm around him and said, "Can a guy buy you a drink on your birthday?" just as the bartender shouted, "Last Call".

When we got home he hugged his mom and called his brother at three am to tell him he loved him. Mary and I sat at the kitchen table and cried. Wished you could have been there Waldo.

RUSTY MCFARLAND

Irish American News
May 2001

Political honchos across Chicago breathed a sigh of relief when Rusty
McFarland died. It's not that they wished him any ill will, it's just that he
would no longer be around to scarf up all their cracked crab, filet mignon,
and jumbo shrimp while draining the bar of everything except beer and
wine at their fundraisers.

Rusty didn't care for parties that served just beer and wine. "I didn't put on
this suit to drink some Heineken and nibble cheeze balls."

Rusty and I traveled the political fundraiser circuit of Chicago for several
years in the late eighties. Sometimes I actually had to buy a ticket, but never
Russ. He was a master at crashing every gala in the city. But it wasn't really
"crashing" in his case. Actually he charmed his way into all of them. He'd
appear at the ticket table like Reginald Van Gleason III and folks just
assumed he was a party regular. And he was, Democrat, Republican,
Larouchie, it made no difference to Russ. I guess that's how he got the nickname, "America's Guest".

Rusty grew up just a few blocks from me on the Southside and his younger
brother Bill was one of my best pals. But I hadn't seen 'ol Russ since child-
hood days when I first ran into him at the beginning of our streak of cocktail party collisions.

"Hey Houli, how's it goin'? Nice party, huh?"

Russ had gotten quite a bit larger since his days of buyin' beer for the kids
at the CK courts. He had probably tripled in weight since then but he carried it well. We started calling him "Gert Frobe" because of his uncanny
resemblance to the late German actor who had starred as 007's nemesis.
Eventually we shortened it to "Goldfinger". He liked that.

He was usually in the company of his sidekick, Gerry Hickey, AKA
"Jerome", "Otis", "Hicks", "the Hickster", "Drool Boy", and a dozen other
arcane Southside nicknames. Jerome had been with the Forest Preserve
District for over twenty years and he had the scoop on every Cook County
Dem cocktail party. "I'm keepin' my ear to the grape vine for you guys!"

Goldfinger and Otis just needed somebody on the eario for Republican fundraisers and since I was then working for Big Jim Thompson I got recruited. I certainly didn't mind because they were great company. However, you could never count on them to join you for a post party refreshment unless you were buyin'. Once the free drinks were gone, so were they.

Rusty spent a lot of time at the racetrack, but he was also working as a private investigator for personal injury attorneys. I asked him how that worked and he said, "I'm kind of like that character Paul Drake on the Perry Mason show." He spent six months in Chicago and six months in Miami. I don't have to tell you which six months.

"In Florida I'm more like Magnum PI."

Goldfinger would call me throughout the summer each week with the low-down on any upcoming banquets and I would tell him what I knew. We hit the Bismarck, Hilton, Sheraton, Navy Pier, Field Museum, Lino's, and dozens of other venues in our search for the best bill of faire that Chicago pols could buy. "I heard there's an Eddie Rosewell party tomorrow night in the Walnut Room." he'd sneer into the phone. "Yeah, but Thompson's having a party at the Drake." I countered. "Forget it, its black tie." He knew, he always knew.

One balmy night there was a huge bash at the Chicago Theatre. Michael Jordan was onstage with those guys from Saturday Night Live who do "Da Bulls, Da Bears!" It was a fundraiser for some disease and the only way in was with a ticket. But Russ heard that there would be a party afterwards in Marshall Fields.

We stationed ourselves outside Fields as the show was ending. There were thousands of people lining the streets hoping to glimpse some of the celebrities and the police had the street blocked with saw horses and mounted cops. I stood at the alley outside with Russ and watched a horse take a piss so powerful that the crowd broke out in applause. Goldfinger said, "That's the most impressive thing I've seen in years."

We tucked in our ties and headed into Fields. Security was heavy and we walked in like we owned the place. A young woman stopped me. "Is your name on the list?" I acted shocked and said, "It better be!" just as Gert Frobe sidled past me to the elevator up to the party. Not one of my names was on the list and I was turned away, but McFarland had used me as a diversion to smile his way into the soiree.

I suddenly felt betrayed and challenged by his expertise. I walked outside to the alley where the stars were entering the building and accosted George Wendt as he passed. George was also an old neighborhood guy and lived two doors down from McFarland when we were kids. "Get me into the party, Rusty McFarland's up there!" It was shameless and pathetic I know, but it worked.

As the elevator doors opened to the party I bolted out in search of Gert Frobe among the luminaries and lobster. He was leaning against a pillar drinking a Rob Roy as he giggled with a gorgeous black model, one of the LuvaBulls. He was in heaven, with a little twinkle on his face and I rushed over to confront him. "Houli, you made it, great!" he said with a wry smile and wink that disarmed me. "Let me introduce you to Tawana. She don't wanna!"

"Thanks for givin' me the slip downstairs Goldfinger, that was some stunt."

Rusty looked perplexed as he guided me toward the bar, "Houli, I thought you knew the rules."

"The rules?"

"I want to thank you for sacrificing yourself on my behalf downstairs at the entrance."

"Are you nuts? I'd never do that."

Goldfinger grinned like a Cheshire cat, "Neither would I Houli. I guess you do know the rules. Try some of the seafood crepes, they're scrumptious."

MY NIGHT WITH RAQUEL

Irish American News
August 2001

I've never met Raquel Welch officially, but one night many years ago two reporters from the National Inquirer offered me $300 bucks to throw a drink in her face.

My wife and I were having dinner at an awards banquet in New York at the Rainbow Room and Ms. Welch was starring on Broadway in WOMAN OF THE YEAR and was there to hype the show. Mary and I weren't exactly at the top of the guest list so we got seated with the troublemakers from the tabloid. Having dinner with folks you've never met before can be awkward, but I have found that a couple of Manhattans help to break the ice.

Just last week I used the same method of becoming fast friends with a group of south siders who I had never met before that night. They had been out at a benefit for Christ the King parish and one of the auction items was dinner with yours truly. Six months later they call me to collect on their purchase and we arranged to meet at Ken's on Western Avenue.

Dawn Joslyn told me she was throwing a birthday party for her husband Mark and I could help them celebrate. She said they would have a group of about six folks, Mark's brother Scott and his wife and some of their friends. I asked her how much they had paid for the honor of dining with me and Dawn said, "I can't remember if it was thirty-five or forty bucks."

I got to Ken's a little bit early to oil up my charm machine and schmoozed with some old pals at the bar. Jack Casto, the proprietor, had thrown in a $100 gift certificate as part of the deal. By the time the Joslyns arrived I was ready to sing for my supper.

They were all in a festive mood and it turned out we had a lot in common, both the Joslyn brothers were fellow alumni of Mt. Carmel and their wives and friends shared stories about their Irish families, theatre in Chicago, sports, and our kids. Scott and Mark own a construction company and I do commercials for the brick industry so I bored them with my views of synthetic stucco vs. brick. We broke bread, cracked jokes, and had a blast. They were wonderful people.

I had asked Frankie Moran to stop in around ten-thirty to rescue me in case the night was a disaster. But when Mo came over to the table and told me, "You've got a phone call at the bar." I was having too much fun to leave.

It reminded me of that night at the Rainbow Room when I got to laughing with the guys from the Inquirer about Raquel and Tommy Tune making their grand entrance. Tommy was an eight-foot tall tap dancer-director who floated across the Rainbow Room escorting the star of the show.

As the paparazzi buzzed about them, and the flash bulbs exploded, I jokingly said, "I'd love to walk right up there and toss this drink in her face and say, "You bitch, Tommy's mine!"

That's when one of the reporters said, "I'll give you $300 bucks right now if you do." And his sidekick countered, "$350!" My wife grabbed my arm and said, "No, he's just kidding." And I said, "Come on you guys, that won't even cover my bail money."

If the lovely Mary wasn't with me that night I'd probably still be in jail for that stunt. I'm the type of guy who needs a chaperone, that little angel who taps me on the shoulder and says, "Are you nuts?"

I got home very late the night of my dinner with the south side Joslyns. My wife met me in the kitchen as I sneaked in the door. "Are you nuts? Forty bucks for the charity and you spend six hours with a bunch of people you don't even know?"

"I know them now. And besides, I don't see anybody paying to have dinner with you!"

"You did!"

"Oh man did I. I paid big time. And I'm still payin!"

So thanks for the dinner Joslyns. I'm sorry you didn't get to meet the lovely Mary. Of course if I had brought her with me that night I wouldn't have stayed quite so long. Or told those dirty jokes in front of the ladies, or soaked up all that booze on your check. Or hung around Ken's after you left until Mary called on the phone and told them to send me home.

Actually maybe you guys are sorry she wasn't there as well. She keeps me out of trouble. Just ask Raquel.

MIDNIGHT MASS STREAKER

Irish American News
December 2001

When Ernie O'Laughlin "streaked" midnight mass on Christmas Eve many years ago at St. Gertrude's parish, he became a folk hero to the North side Irish. At least that's the way I heard it the other night in a bar in Forest Park.

A guy on the next stool told me the story. He said he was speaking on the condition of "anonymity". You hear that a lot lately on the news. It's a good way to cover your butt in case people find out you are full of malarkey.

So take this story with a grain or two of rock salt. According to my source it happened in the early '70's and over the years I'm sure Ernie's reputation has grown along with the details of his fabled adventure. It may be apocryphal but it certainly put me in the Christmas spirit.

It was a blizzardy Christmas Eve and Ernie and his pals were driving around celebrating. They had started early that afternoon after some last minute shopping. The carload of North side Irish lads were in high school and still in the midst of teenage rebellion.

Ernie made up for his small stature with a daredevil spirit that his friends loved to exploit. As they pulled up in front of St. Gert's on Glenwood one of the guys said, "Hey Ernie, $50 bucks says you don't have the guts to streak midnight mass."

Ten beers into his twelve pack; Ernie was never one to turn down a challenge and immediately stripped down to only his shoes, and got ready to step into the history books. He pulled a ski mask over his head and leaped from the car at a full gallop. "Pick me up on Granville in thirty seconds."

The choir was just hitting the high note on "Oh Holy Night" when the back doors burst open and a skinny, naked teenager sprinted down the middle aisle joining the congregation as he shrieked "Oh night Diviiiiine!" He took a left in front of the altar and fell on his keester, but bounced back up again to dash out the exit by the statue of the Blessed Mother.

Most of the folks at mass were too stunned to move. Many couldn't believe what they had just witnessed. Some of the kids began to snicker but the members of the Holy Name Society were outraged and several of those Irish turkey birds had smoke coming out of their ears as they jumped from their pews and gave chase.

Ernie's heart was pounding louder than the hoof beat of the Irishmen in pursuit. He hit the crash bar on the door in front of the altar to Mary and he could swear she smiled at him as he burst into the cold to meet his pals.

They were not there.

The carload of young Micks laughed as they sped away and left poor 'lil Ernie O'Laughlin naked in the snow. Ernie heard shouts of "blasphemy" over his shoulder and saw seven or eight incensed old country Irish plumbers ready to disconnect his flamshooter.

O'Laughlin took off like a rocket, running for his life. His youth, his bravado, and the fact that he was naked helped him spring like a gazelle with the lions in hunt. He zigzagged through yards and down alleys through the moonlit snowy night. Still they kept coming, "The little bugger is on Estes avenue."

Ernie was freezing and scared as he jogged through McCarthy's front yard. A floodlight hit him in his face and he figured the jig was up. But no orders were given as he cowered there in nude surrender.

He put his hands in front of the O'Laughlin family jewels and stepped meekly forward, farther into the light. There was no one there, except a life size crèche that had brought Mrs. McCarthy glory in the Altar Guild Society. Mary and Joseph knelt by the crib over the baby Jesus and there were cows and sheep and even three huge guys on ceramic camels.

Ernie grabbed the shawl from the shoulders of the Mary statue and knelt as if a poor shepherd boy at the Nativity. He felt self conscious among the statues and looked at the face of the Blessed Mother, still a teenager herself. She would understand. Ernie didn't mean nothing bad by it, he's just a kid, in swaddling clothes trying to escape the IRA.

Ernie started praying', "Oh I'm so sorry Blessed Mother, please get me outta this and I will never, never, never come to church naked again. I was just tryin' to re-live my baptism." He looked up and thought Mary was smiling at him, laughing.

"You better get out of here Ernie."

It seemed like good advice and Ernie took off on angels' wings. It was Ernie's Christmas miracle. He got home and the one thing his pals did was to stick with his alibi.

My new friend on the bar stool threw back another shot of Bushmills and said, "And today he is Cardinal Ernie O'Laughlin."

"Yeah, right," I said, "I suppose he's the Cardinal of Bethlehem, Pennsylvania."

"No, he's a coach for the St. Louis Cardinals. But that's another story."

I threw a couple bucks on the bar and wished my friend a Happy Holidays.

The next day I called St. Gertrude's rectory to get confirmation of the incident from the pastor Father Bill Kanneally.

"I wasn't there at the time, but yes, I've heard that story myself. We don't have a midnight mass on Christmas Eve anymore. We start mass at 10:30 PM now and those kind of antics are the main reason. I'm certainly glad that "streaking" has died down."

I asked Father Bill if he thought the story was true and he chuckled, "St. Gertrude's has a long mythology."

So to the folks at St. Gertrude's, to Father Bill Kanneally, to my flapjaw friend at the bar, and to the Irish all over Chicago, North side, West side, South side, and especially to you Cardinal Ernie O'Laughlin, I say, "Merry Christmas."

CHAPTER SIX

2002

TRICK SHOP RILEY

Irish American News
March 2002

Got a shock one night a few weeks ago when I was perusing the Irish scratch sheet, the obituaries. Jim Riley, owner of Riley's Trick Shop, had finally kicked the bucket at the ripe old age of 93. The Trib ran a photo with the obit and he looked like the same old wisenheimer that used to razz us kids whenever we visited his shop back in the '50's and '60's.

I bought my first fake dog poop at Riley's, as well as the old fly in the ice cube, hand buzzers, and several whoopee cushions. We started riding our bikes to Riley's on Saturdays when I was about ten years old. His shop was on 79th Street then and it was a long journey for us kids from 95th Street, but the inventory of corny gadgets kept us rapt for hours afterwards.

On Saturdays the place would be packed with kids cracking up over all the goofy stuff on sale. Riley wouldn't toss you out either. He knew that sooner or later every kid in that store was going to buy something to bring home and embarrass the family. Even if you had a meager allowance you could always afford cigarette "loads." These tiny white slivers of TNT were then inserted into the Lucky Strike of unsuspecting Uncle Charlie. When he lit up his smoke the thing would explode and practically give him a heart attack. Great fun!

As I entered my teens, Riley moved his trick shop over to 91st and Western, right next to Jim's Bicycle Shop. I'm sure plenty of kids in my parish said a silent prayer each night thanking Riley for making himself so convenient. You could check out the new bikes at Jim's and then saunter into Riley's for some sure fire amusement. He had a wall on the left that was covered with rubber masks of every variety, from Khrushchev to the Devil, and plenty of grotesque monsters with eyeballs dangling.

On the right wall up top were the plastic buttocks and boxes and boxes of wacky contraptions, all of them catalogued by Riley. There was something a little bit racy about Riley's, at least to my young eyes. The jokes and tricks were often scatological and those vulgarities just made our gang laugh harder. I once bought a wanted poster at Riley's and hung it in my garage until my Dad made me take it down. It offered a $500 reward for some mope pictured on the poster who was guilty of "booger picking".

The last time I remember visiting Riley's was right before leaving the old neighborhood for college. I wanted something outrageous to decorate my dorm room and knew exactly where to find it. Riley had a machine that printed fake headlines on a newspaper. It was a very popular gimmick. Riley's wife told me to spell out the headline I wanted on a piece of paper, no more than 28 letters. I wracked my brain for something obscene to print that would greet my new roommate when he walked in the door. Two bucks spent at Riley's Trick Shop could leave an impression that would last a lifetime.

When I handed her the paper, she balked. By today's standards my headline would be every day patter on Leno or Letterman but back in 1967 it seemed crude and tasteless. She called Riley out from the back of the shop and handed him the note with my proposed headline. He looked at it and laughed, and then said, "Print it." He turned to me and squinted through his glasses, "You're a sick kid, ever think about going into the joke business?"

Thirty-five years later I'm in the joke business and Riley is shaking hands with St. Peter. I hope he is using one of his old hand buzzers. God Bless you Riley.

TINY & WANDA

Irish American News
April 2002

Tiny Brogan and Wanda Taylor were destined for each other as the poets say.

Wanda was an ambitious nineteen year old who met Tiny on Western Avenue one fateful night when she waved to him as he slowed down in his Cadillac and sweetly chirped, "Hi, wanna date?"

She didn't mind that Tiny was in his late forties. She felt he just had that much more to offer. She also didn't seem to mind that Tiny weighed over 375 pounds.

Tiny had just come from Skip's New Evergreen Tavern where he had cashed his check from the Sanitary District. He was flush and half in the bag and Wanda was just what he was looking for that moonlit night.

Romance blossomed and soon Tiny was driving down to 67th and Western every payday to look for his new friend Wanda. Wanda would giggle when she saw Tiny's black Fleetwood glide into the spot in front of Gillespie's car dealership.

Sometimes she was busy with another customer. But Tiny would wait, smoking a cigar and listening to the oldies station. Wanda wasn't like most of the girls Tiny had met in his life, snotty Beverly bitches who wouldn't give him the time of day. Wanda was different. She made Tiny feel like a king. He was falling in love.

Tiny became one of Wanda's regulars and she started looking forward to seeing his beefy, smiling face behind the wheel each week after he cashed his check.

And then one night Tiny was late. Wanda worried, it was almost two am and Tiny still hadn't arrived for his date. But Wanda's favorite fella had a good excuse. He won $500 bucks on a scratch-off ticket and had gone to a Hawks game to celebrate with some pals. That night Tiny consumed nine hot dogs and gallons of Miller Lites at the United Center. He felt like he was ready to burst as he cruised Western Avenue in search of little Wanda.

Wanda's heart leapt as she saw Tiny screech to a halt in front of her. She was ready to scold her big boy until she saw the C-note slapped on his forehead and Tiny told her he wanted to share his winnings with his little darling. They parked in the dark of a cross street and got comfy.

Tiny was so in love at that very moment that his heart just burst with emotion. He had a vision of Elysium right before he slumped over on top of Wanda, deader than Kelsey's nuts.

Now Wanda was in a pickle. She was stuck under Tiny's huge girth and her diminutive frame was trapped within the folds of Tiny's fat. He must have weighed four times 'lil Wanda and she just couldn't budge him. Wanda lay there for hours trying to lift Tiny Brogan but the best she could do was reach down and empty his wallet of the rest of his scratch off winnings.

She had a lot of explaining to do when two cops showed up that morning to investigate the black Caddy with the motor running.

Eddie Dunn and Jim McGonnigle were on duty that day and they both recognized Tiny's car even before they shined their flashlights into his fat, dead, hairy ass.

They had both grown up with Tiny and were shocked and saddened by his sudden demise. They were even more shocked when they heard Wanda's voice squeak for help from below.

Eddie lifted Tiny's shoulders while McGonnigle pulled up Tiny's pants and freed Wanda for the post mortem. Wanda explained how Tiny was her boyfriend forever and how they loved each other, but the cops were skeptical.

They agreed with Wanda that Tiny was a wonderful guy. They also agreed that Tiny would want her taken care of, so they pinched her for prostitution.

Wanda spent the next night in the Gresham lockup. She got released on an I-bond the next morning and walked into the sunshine. She waited for the Halsted street bus and thought about how she missed Tiny.

Suddenly a kid dashed up behind her, lurched Wanda's purse off her shoulder and sprinted into traffic. Wanda gave chase, screaming at the villain, ran into the rushing path of a northbound bus, and was flattened by the front end.

Officers Eddie Dunn and Jim McGonnigle filled out the accident report. Little Wanda was dead.

Now a cynic could say that was poetic, and a preacher might say they both got what they deserved, but Eddie Dunn was a romantic. All he said was, "Looks like Tiny and Wanda will be together forever now."

TOM REARDON

Irish American News
August 2002

I was relaxing in the back of a taxi about fifteen years ago, shooting the breeze with cabbie Mohammed Yaktoff when he ran the light at Randolph and Jefferson and a Buick creamed us coming through the intersection.

They took me to Cabrini Hospital and the Indian nurse in ER thought I was drunk. But it was actually the effect of that LeSabre knocking my noggin all over the back of Mohammed's cab. Later that night I lay in the hospital bed while little birds chirped in circles around my head.

A guy walked in with mustard on his tie, a huge gut, and a stethoscope around his neck. "Hey, your brother Willy called me, asked me to check up on you."

He looked like he had just gotten off the bar stool ten minutes ago and he started shining a pen light into my eyeballs.

My noodle was still half scrambled and my brother Willy has had some wacko pals in his lifetime so I was leery. He put his hand on my shoulder and peered into my eyes. This guy ain't no doctor, he looks like a cop, sort of an Irish Columbo. I smelled a rat.

"Are you really a doctor?"

"Of course I'm a doctor, what the hell do you think I am? I'm Dr. Reardon."

I wasn't really hurt that bad, according to Reardon, "You just got your bell rung, that's all."

Fate put me in Mohammed's cab that night and meeting Tom Reardon was better than winning the lottery.

Tom Reardon, "Reemsy" to his pals, became my doctor and my friend. He wasn't like most sawbones. When I went for my follow-up a week later at St. Joe's I saw him standing in front of the hospital sneakin' a smoke.

He was always late. I used to schedule my appointment last of the day because we could glide over to the Hinky Dink bar in the basement of Marshall Fields to discuss my medical history.

You never felt awkward if you were overweight and a lousy specimen of health because so was he. He made his patients comfortable that way. You were in good hands.

He was a south side kid blessed with a brain. Some say we don't have many of 'em, so when God calls a gifted Southside guy with extraordinary wisdom, we must salute him.

Reemsy grew up in Back of the Yards and then moved to Barnabas when he started at Iggy. His talents were developed, as many great Irishmen were, at Notre Dame. He went onto Stritch Loyola Medical School and interned at Cook County, where he married nurse Monica Metzger. He showed her the Irish way.

As a Lieutenant Commander in the Navy, Reemsy was the medical officer on the USS Vermillion. The Chief woke him up one night because he figured the ship's doctor should handle this problem. "There's a roach in the mess hall." Reemsy did not like his sleep disturbed and walked over, pulled out his service revolver and shot the roach.

He performed an emergency appendectomy on the high seas, and he had never performed surgery before. He read the book. One of the many lives ol' Reemsy saved.

When he went into practice his client list was the creme de la creme of Southside hooligans. Reemsy was my old man's doc and he lived to be 91, cussing and fighting til the end, thanks to Tom Reardon.

I got Reemsy to invest in show biz once. He lost his dough and he never beefed. But he did remark to me after the next prostate exam, "Now we're even."

He was sick for years but wouldn't talk about it. The last time I saw him was White Sox opening day. I was walking along the concourse and spotted him, wearing his trench coat, standing in line for the pisser with a beer in one hand and a smoke in the other. He said, "You caught me doin' everything."

He was at the game with Johnny Lattner, Red Kerr, and Ed Doody and he was havin' a blast. He must've known then that his time was short.

When he was dying' in the hospital his longtime pal Jimmy Cull kept visiting.

Jimmy said, "Tom, if I'm an annoyance just let me know."

Reemsy said, "Jimmy, you've been an annoyance your whole damn life."

Tom and Monica raised their kids Liam, Tom, Erin, and Colleen in Sauganash. At his funeral were all the folks whose lives Tom had touched, the Basilica was packed. One of the kids entitled her eulogy, "A Beautiful Mind". She once asked her dad "Who was the greatest person you ever met?" and Reemsy said, "Your mother."

They don't come any smarter than that on the south side. Reemsy, we'll miss ya 'ol pal, ya went too soon.

Irish American News
September 2002

CLOUT CITY

Chicago clout can be a precious commodity, better than good looks and even money. Those who wield it have no idea how really sweet it can be for those on whom it is bestowed. Clout is at it's most delicious when delivered alongside a squad car with it's blue lights flashing or at the end of a very, very long line. But the consummate clout can only be found in a Cook County courtroom.

Mike "Oats" McNeal told me his favorite clout story over a few beers a few weeks ago. Mike told me, "It was one of the greatest moments I've ever had in my life." He's a natural born storyteller and as he spun his yarn he reminded me of Sylvester the cat, after all those blunders, he had finally devoured Tweety bird.

Oats was driving on the Southside some thirty years ago, he had just left a tavern at closing and his pal said, "Follow me to the Blue Moon, they're open all night." Sure you've been in his shoes, you're following another car to a destination and you don't want to lose them. As Oats cruised down 99th street towards the entrance to Route 57 at Halsted, he zipped through a stoplight as it hit gold, not because he was imprudent, but he didn't want to lose that car in front of him and the opportunity to finish his evening in another saloon.

As soon as he got through the light, down the street comes a squad car and pulls him over. This is the moment many of us dread, just you and the copper, a few hours before dawn breaks on a desolate street in Chicago.

The young cop got out of the car and told Mike he ran the red light.

"Well look officer, I'm following this guy and I'm sure it was yellow."Oats looked in him in the eye hoping to find compassion.

"We're the only 3 cars out here at 4AM, can't you give me a pass?"

The copper says, "I'm going to have to issue you a citation."

This is when Oats overstepped the bounds of good etiquette. "Well you're a real frickin' Dudley Doowright, aren't ya?"

The policeman was not pleased with this remark. Oats says, "Oh, he got hot, his face was beet red, and he gave me the ticket."

Considering the situation, the hour, and the number of beers consumed I would say Oats was lucky. But he got even luckier.

A few weeks later he showed up at 321 North LaSalle Street for traffic court. The young cop showed up too, with fire in his eyes.

Mike's eyes were twinkling as he told me the story. "This cop is readin' the riot act to the judge, blah, blah, blah, he wants me to hang for it, and the judge sez, 'Is that all officer?' Cop sez, 'Yes, your honor.

Judge says 'thank you' turns to me and sez, 'Hey Mike, howya doin'? How's the old man?"

Sometimes when your clout kicks in, its like getting high-fived by St. Peter at the pearly gates.

The judge was the honorable Nicholas J. Boling, (known in some circles as Nick the Nose), former alderman of the 7th Ward where Mike grew up in South Shore. The fix wasn't in; it was just the joyful recognition of a guy from the old neighborhood.

Mike's smile was incandescent as he remembered the scene. "The judge says, 'Well, tell your old man I said hi.', and he turns to the cop and says, 'I think we'll give this one a pass, what do you think officer?' And the cop says, 'Yes, your honor'. Judge Nick sez, 'Case dismissed.' and I turn to the cop with this grin on my face and said, "Thank you!""

Even Sylvester could afford to be polite at that point. The old neighborhood had clouted him home.

Muckrakers have besmirched the reputation of clout by mixing it up with scandal, bribes, and chicanery. But clout is merely an expression of good will. It might be delivered with a wink and a nod, but so are many expressions of good will, like toasting a relative or family friend, helping someone find a job, or donating to a worthy cause.

In the city that works, clout is the finest fuel of all. It's the raised glass across the room to the man of the hour. It's the double sawbuck in the paw of the doorman at the Palmer House. It's the Tweetie Pie eatin' grin on the face of Oats McNeal as he thanked that young copper in traffic court.

A BRIDGEPORT FABLE

Irish American News
December 2002

As Christmas stories go, it ain't a pretty one. Mike Boyle had an irritable bowel. He'd lived on a diet of Harrington's and Guinness for years and those elixirs took their toll on Mike's keester just in time for the holidays.

Mike's wife Kiki would pick out his pants at Marshall's. She'd confide to the sales girl, "My husband is kind of hard to shop for. He craps his pants a lot."

Mike would lose control at the most embarassing moments. He once started laughing really hard at his daughter Rosie's christening and it triggered an explosion in his gabardines. Gaelic Park cleared out fast after that incident.

Mike tells me some war stories. "It happened once when I was walking across the bridge to Michigan Avenue, another time on my way up to communion at St. Gabe's, and once in the waiting room at Jiffy Lube."

"But the absolutely worst time was when I played Santa Claus at the 11th Ward Christmas party."

Shakespearians would say Mike Boyle's performance was odorous that day. The Alderman and Mayor were scheduled to attend and Mike would hand out presents to the kids. It was a sweet gig, a c-note and a vacation day from his city job.

He was nervous about meeting the heavy clout that Christmas Eve and stopped by Schaller's around noon. Mike slammed three shots of Goldshlager with his luncheon beers. He wasn't cockeyed, just wanted a little bracer, but it turned into a bowl 'o gravy in Santa's trousers.

Everything had gone fine until right after they all sang Rudolph the Red Nosed Reindeer. Mike took his position in a royal chair and the kids filed through the line.

A ten-year-old kid named Frankie Riley had jumped into his lap, showing off for his pals. "Santa I want money!" Boyle caught the kid and let go of everything else. Uh oh, boys and girls, Kris Kringle just made kaka.

Nobody noticed at first, except Mike of course. He knew it would just be a matter of minutes before somebody caught a whiff of his "accident". Sweat formed under his beard and he eyed Daley and the big shots making their way to Santa for a photo op. He saw his job with Streets and Sanitation going up in smoke. Mike bolted for the door saying, "Gotta check the reindeer."

He threw some newspaper on the front seat of his Chevy and sped home to Kiki. Snow had fallen and the roads were icy but not as slippery as that Lumina's driver seat. The humiliation was evident on Mike's face when Kiki opened the kitchen door. "Oh no Mike, not again!"

Kiki helped Mike clean himself up that Christmas Eve. He was incon-
solable, but she was his loving wife. "Oh you poor man. I'll wash out your
pants. I just hope the costume shop will take them back."

After some wet naps and tears Mike was able to sit at the kitchen table and
crack open a beer. He still had his beard and red jacket on with a clean pair
of tidy whities. He poured his heart out to Kiki and declared his enduring
love for her because she always stood by him when he misfired. He was
naughty, she was nice.

Christmas now has new meaning for Mike and Kiki. Their love of twenty
some years was solidified by Mike's calamity. He stays close to home during the holiday season now and stopped wearing khaki's years ago.

He sent word back through the ward that he had taken ill that day, food poisoning, and he didn't want to embarrass the Mayor, or unleash his nerve gas
on the innocent children.

Bridgeporters chuckled at Mike's mishap and the kids never forgot the year
of the stinky Santa Claus. Ever since that Christmas season, folks in the 11th
Ward have called Mike Boyle "Shanta".

CHAPTER SEVEN

2003

THE VIRGIN BARTENDER

Irish American News
February 2003

I was driving my son Bill to work the other day when he blurted out a confession. He's been tending bar at Skelly & Skelly on Madison Street in Forest Park and really loves his job, but his conscience was now bothering him and he told me his troubles.

"I had to throw an old lady out of the bar yesterday."

Well, that's one more thing we have in common. If you tend bar for any length of time you're going to eventually have an encounter with the dreaded drunken old lady. They're the most dangerous breed of boozer. They lull you into security like a sleeping crocodile on the riverbank and then before you know it, their jaws are snapping around your neck and you are toast.

Skelly & Skelly's just opened around the holidays and it's a swell place for a beer and a burger. Brothers Mike and Scott bought the old Upper Deck and renovated that worn out gin mill into a comfortable classy joint. If you drop in, make sure you lay a nice big tip on the bartender Billy. That way he won't be hitting me up for dough.

Bill tells me he was working an afternoon shift when in walked Mrs. McGillicuddy, three sheets to the wind. He had watched her stagger in the door and assumed wrongly her cockeyed gait was a result of old age. She surveyed the room like a rattlesnake pickin' its target and snapped at Billy, "Gimme a Tanqueray and tonic. Where's the old bar?"

The old bar may have catered to that clientele and the lads at Skelly's have discovered that when you open a new bar on the strip, your very first customers are usually those who've been banned everywhere else. Mrs. McGillicuddy wasn't interested in exchanging niceties with my son and within minutes he was pouring her drink into a paper cup so she couldn't smash it against the wall. This resulted in her spewing a stream of vituperative vowels as he grabbed her purse and escorted her to the door.

Ten minutes later she walked back in with no memory of her last visit and shouted "Gimme a Tanqueray and tonic!"

Billy told me they kicked her out again and sent her down to Horan's. If Aeneas was there that day he'd have asked her to dance.

My son's guilt over throwing an old lady out of the bar was a direct result of his respect for her age. He told me, "She's probably been boozin' for more years than I've been alive, and I'm the one cuttin' her off?" I knew the feeling.

I told Billy about my first encounter with a drunken old lady. It was many years ago in Rockaway Beach, New York, at the grand opening of the Houli-Dooley, which I owned with the late Pete Dooley.

A matronly lady came into the bar and introduced herself. She was very sweet, sort of Rockaway's version of Aunt Bea. "Oh boys, I wish you all the luck in the world. I'm Mrs. Z, everybody in the neighborhood knows me. I'm having flowers sent over for your grand opening today. Gimme a Fleischman's and soda."

We thanked Mrs. Z and served her the drink. The Z was short for something like Ziolokowski, but her ensuing transformation at the bar brought the names Jekyll and Hyde to mind.

Within an hour she had consumed several more Fleischman's and soon was screaming at the top of her lungs into the ear of the lady on the next stool, a Mrs. Cronin from Roscommon. I asked Mrs. Z to lower her voice and she promptly told me to "Shut the f......up. I'm Mrs. Z!"

Mrs. Z then tried to punch Mrs. Cronin in the face as she pulled on her hair. Our grand opening was now officially up for grabs. My partner Pete Dooley and I grabbed Mrs. Z and moved her towards the door. She wasn't about to go without a fight and kept screaming, "I'm Mrs. Z! I'm Mrs. Z!"

Pete grabbed her legs and I had her flailing midsection as we got to the door. At that very moment, and I swear this is true, a floral delivery guy walked through the door and said, "I've got flowers for you guys from a Mrs. Z."

We tossed Mrs. Z out into the street, shoved her floral arrangement into the back room, and put her name at the top of what would soon become a very long list.

I'm sure Skelly & Skelly's has a similar list. And I'm also sure that Mrs. McGillicuddy's name is on it.

As I dropped Billy off at work that day I told him not to feel guilty about throwing the old lady out of the bar and added words of fatherly advice, "You'll never forget your first one."

BILLY'S BLIND FAITH

Irish American News
April 2003

I was riding the El to work a few months back with my sons Bill and Paddy. We pick up the Green Line at Harlem and ride it through the west side to the Loop. The train rumbles through the heart of the ghetto and you can encounter some interesting folk.

On this particular day a preacher got on at Pulaski. He started his spiel about how he helped drug-addicted and troubled brothers and sisters at his church and he was doing a little fundraising for his charitable work. He then produced a small, white letter size envelope and said, "In this envelope are three sacred cloths, they have been anointed with mystical powers and will grant your prayers."

I asked the Reverend, "Who anointed them?"

"Ah did."

He then made his pitch, the envelope with the three cloths, one blue, one red, one pink, was yours for a donation of only one dollar. A big basketball player sittin' near us said, "Let's see what they look like?"

But the street corner minister would not exhibit the goods. They were, after all anointed. Nobody bought one and he moved to the next car.

Later than night I sat in front of the TV with Bill and Paddy and we laughed about the guy and his routine. Suddenly Bill said, "I've got something I want to show you guys."

Paddy and I looked at each other in puzzlement and Bill returned with a small white envelope. He laughed and said he had bought one from the guy the day before we saw him but was too embarrassed to admit it then. We inspected the envelope.

Inside were three small squares of cheesecloth. "Be careful, these have been anointed."

It appeared that the reverend had bought a couple yards of red, pink, and blue cheesecloth and got out his scissors and started a business. And my son Billy bought one.

Like a good father, I asked Billy, "Are you nuts? You know it's a scam."

Billy smiled, "Yeah, but you never know. I want my prayers to be answered so what the hell."

Paddy lifted one of the cloths to Bill's head, "Smell it, it's got like perfume on it."

Bill was unfazed, "Hey, it was only a buck, and the guy put some effort into it, and maybe he'll use the money to really help somebody."

We handed the cloths around and cracked up, smelling them and rubbing them between our fingers for luck. I was suddenly proud of Bill's blind faith in a man who just showed up one day on the El. For all we know that guy could have been a prophet.

Jesus said, "When you do this for the least of my brethren, you do it for me."

What if we get to heaven and that old black preacher asks us for our tickets. We say, where do you get the tickets? And the Reverend says, "They's little blue, pink, and red squares of cheesecloth, I was sellin' 'em on the Green Line for years."

THE LOVE OF MY LIFE

Irish American News
May 2003

I met this gorgeous lil' Irish chick at an audition for Shakespeare's "All's Well That Ends Well". I was reading for the part of Parolles, the braggart captain, the buffoon. I got the part, typecasting.

When I showed up in Washington for rehearsals, there she was. She was playing Diana and her name was Mary Carney. She gave me the cold shoulder the first couple days. I ran into her one day at the grocery store and beckoned her over to the produce. I pointed to the ripe, succulent fruit and said, "You're some tomato!"

She thought I was crazy.

We started hanging out at The Tune Inn on Capitol Hill after the show. I had a girlfriend back in New York, but I was falling in love with lil' Mary Carney. After the show closed we met for lunch in Gotham a couple times. Then I moved to LA. Lil' Mary Carney came to visit me. She stayed for a week. After I put her on the red eye to go back, I sat in the car in the airport parking lot and realized that I couldn't live without her.

I packed my bags and went back to New York to get her. I took the lovely Mary to Chicago to meet my family. They loved her instantly. My mom gave me a ring given to her by my dad. It was in a tiny box and she winked. When we returned to Gotham I got down on my knee, layed the ring on lil' Mary Carney and asked her, "Will you be mine in apple blossom time?"

I met Mary's mother the day before the wedding. Margaret was a widow and hit town from upstate New York with her eight other Carney kids. Mary's dad, Dr. Ted Carney, had died when she was in high school. By the time I met her family it was too late for lil' Mary to back out of the deal.

We had the rehearsal dinner at O'Lunney's on 44th Street. My dad got half-bagged and sang at the piano, "And the nickels and the dimes rolled away." Mary sang "Danny Boy", and there wasn't a dry eye at the party. I woke up the next morning face down on the floor in my best man Jack Whalen's hotel room. I felt like someone had boiled my face. Jack's wife Jean looked down at me and said, "You better get outta here, today is your wedding day!"

We got married at St. Malachy's on 49th Street, "the Actor's Chapel." After the wedding, the guests marched down 8th Avenue and over 44th Street behind the bagpiper. The hookers and winos on the street were cheering.

The reception was at Sardi's, a showbiz folk landmark. I bumped into Carol Channing as I was coming out of the men's room there one day. The wedding party took over the Club Room on the second floor, buffet tables and open bar baby. We partied there and then I brought the gang back to our bridal suite at the Plaza.

Jack Whalen tossed a champagne bucket out the window that crashed onto Central Park South. The wedding party was now officially out of control. Lil' Mary Carney started to cry. "Who are these people from the south side of Chicago?"

That was May 28, 1978, twenty-five years ago. Now she knows who they are. She knows the roller coaster ride with this Hooligan can be scary, full of thrills and chills. She knows the pain of childbirth, (twins the natural way), and the pride of raising two fine young men named Bill and Paddy. She knows my 401K plan is a Lotto ticket. And I hope she knows how much I love her. Happy Anniversary lil' Mary Carney.

7TH INNING STRETCH

Irish American News
September 2003

How bout them White Sox? I've got the fever. Man, I hope they are still winning when this paper hits the streets. They're making it a great summer for this fan.

I was laying on my couch last month when the fever came over me. The Sox were on TV and I said to myself, "I got to get out there to a game." Then I had a revelation. I could probably BS my way into Sox Park as a "journalist". Yeah, I could get great seats, free seats, and the royal treatment in the press box. Why hadn't I thought of this before? It was so simple yet thrilling, like sneaking into the game.

I called the Sox press office the next day and started throwin'. Katie Kirby was the press rep and she bought the whole bit, found me a guy to interview and set me up with a Full Access Media badge. I could go anywhere in the park, except the ladies room.

Charlie Carey was hosting one of his infamous lunches at Gene & Georgetti's on game day. He had Pat Duff and Dan Henning with us at the table. Give these guys knives and forks and get out of their way. Lions chomping on Wildebeest couldn't do more damage. The steaks, chicken, and antipasto would lay the foundation for a great night.

Head Sheahan dropped me off at Sox Park later that day. I picked up my press pass and felt like Jack Brickhouse. My interview was over by 4:30 and the game didn't start til 7. What to do? I held off having my first beer until 6 and roamed around the ballpark. The Sox were playing the A's that night and I watched the first five innings from the press box.

I met the Head and Frankie Moran over by a beer stand at the top of the sixth. The Sox were kicking butt and my fever was high. My pals kept warning me that they shut off beer sales in the seventh inning so I started pounding. That's when my Sox fever sort of turned into flu like symptoms. I felt that familiar rumble in my gut and knew I was in trouble.

As the guys handed me my last beer I glanced over at the men's room. It was now the middle of the seventh and there were about eight hundred guys in line to tinkle. Nature was calling me in a bigger way and I squeezed my cheeks together and got in line.

Sweat broke out on my forehead as I inched my way up in the line in front of a stall. The door opened in front of me just as I was starting my sixth Hail Mary. I hustled in and was greeted with the rented beer the slobs left all over the seat. I gave it a quick rub down and plopped. I made it!

There was a line of about twenty guys waiting at my door. When the next mope in line saw my feet take the number two position he screamed. "He's takin' a dump!"

The entire mens room groaned and began shuffling into other lines for more speedy access. I yelled back, "That's right, and I'm taking my time!"

I could hear them grumbling while I rested in the rest room. They should be thankful I got here in time or they'd really have something to gripe about. I had nothing to read so I finished my business and tidied up. When I opened the door there were fifty guys giving me the evil eye. "Sorry guys, but that was brutal."

I got no respect in spite of the press pass still dangling from my neck. I left them to wash my hands with a smirk on my face. As I departed the men's room I said, "Watch out for that Sox fever, it could be contagious!"

The Sox won that night too. I'm going to try and get to more games this season but next time I'm wearing a diaper. Go Sox!

I'VE HAD SOME WORK DONE

Irish American News
November 2003

I've tried to make a career out of being a wise ass, and a couple weeks ago it all caught up with me.

You see I had some plastic surgery done, a little nip and tuck of the interior of my butt.

Some folks have told me I spend too much time talking about this stuff. So maybe it's poetic justice that I had a colonoscopy and some hemmie surgery two weeks ago.

I can't promise I'll never talk of it again, but hopefully I can put this subject to rest with this public service message.

Colon cancer has killed a lot of guys my age. After the age of fifty most doctors recommend an annual colonoscopy. Without getting too scientific the procedure involves sliding a tube up your rectum and taking a look inside your colon. Calling it a tube could be misleading; it's probably more like a telescope.

I'd been putting it off for years because.... well I just didn't like the idea of a telescope being up there. But I was also having some other problems in that area thanks to my Irish ancestors.

The doc told me "piles" are mostly hereditary and some members of my family have inherited a bundle. I've had hemmies for at least ten years now but within the last year they got really...really bad, —I had my very own shrimp cocktail hanging out of my keester.

Actually they were more embarrassing than they were painful because the bleeding got so bad that I had to abandon light colored trousers and for the last six months I was often wearing an ass-kotex, a home made device of wadded up toilet paper to protect my gabardines.

There were several occasions when it would slip down my pants leg and appear on the floor of an office where I would be conducting some high level conference. "Excuse me Mike, I think you dropped something."

Indeed I did.

And so I decided to take arms against a sea of troubles, and by opposing, end them. And while you're up there doc, give me the colonoscopy.

So I went under the knife, but not without some trepidation. I heard horror stories of botched hemmie jobs. "Yeah, the doc screwed up, it was coming out like spaghetti so she wound up having to crap through her ear for the rest of her life!"

It was first time surgery for me and I was scared shitless. I asked the doc about that story as I lay waiting to get knocked out. He said, "I'm not gonna screw it up." And yes I believed him.

I went to sleep under a general anesthetic and didn't feel a thing. And with the colonoscopy you can just get up and go home.

But I had some infrastructure work done so of course when I woke up I felt like the Titanic had just passed through my anal canal. For the next week I was on Vicodin, and that is some good stuff, but still every time I sat on the toilet I felt like I was giving birth... to King Kong.

But I survived, call it character building. The doc told me it was a good thing I had the scope because he found five polyps on my colon and snipped those babies off while he was there. If it weren't for the hemmies the whole operation would have been a breeze. And to top it off, I am the proud owner of a brand new anus.

A week or so after the surgery I visited the doc for a follow up. Doctor Jim opened his folder and showed me a Polaroid. "This is your colon."

Swell, not only had the guy been up my ass but he took some snapshots while he was up there.

How do I know that photo is authentic? It's not like I'm going to recognize my own colon. I've never been one to use a rear view mirror. The doc could be using that same picture on every patient. "Yeah, Denise, put his charts on the table and I'm gonna need the colon photo too."

It could have been a photograph of an animal's colon, I wouldn't know. So I just went along with it. He didn't really give me that good a look at the pics, opened the folder, pointed out my colon, "and this is the hemorrhoid", and snapped it shut.

But the polyps were non-cancerous and I am clean. Thank you God.

I'm not interested in being the poster boy for rectal surgery but I do want to encourage men my age to have the colonoscopy. It might save your life and it will definitely give you and your family peace of mind. My plumbing is working like new and the best advice I'd like to give all you guys are the prophetic words my old man used to always say to me, "Watch your ass."

THE NEXT KING OF ENGLAND

Irish American News
December 2003

By now you've heard the stories coming out of Buckingham Palace and servant George Smith's claim to having been buggered by a member of Bonnie Prince Charlie's staff. Not exactly a big surprise.

I might not be royalty but I'd know enough not to bend over in Windsor's house. Evidently the butlers in that joint have more than a stiff upper lip.

Is the Prince of Wales responsible for this behavior? I have to admit I'm baffled. If I were the next king of England I wouldn't be surrounding myself with pansies and dating the ugliest woman in the United Kingdom.

I'm sure Camilla Parker Bowles is charming but she's got a face like Man 'o War. Charles must have been dropped on his crown when he was a baby. How else can you explain that goofy perspective on life and his ears flappin' in the breeze by the Thames.

Last month the rumors got worse as the monarchy tried to stop newspapers from printing the allegations of sexual contact between Prince Charles and Michael Fawcett, one of his closest advisors. Supposedly one of the servants walked in on the two while Fawcett gave Charles some tips on properly mounting a polo pony.

It all started when former palace butler Paul Burrell began publicizing his new book, A Royal Duty. Hey Paul, a royal pain is more like it. Who knew wearing a saddle was part of the job description, eh ol' chum?

Nobody is really surprised at any of this; I mean Brits have been practicing the art of poofery ever since Stonehenge. Let's not forget that the last Prince of Wales abdicated his throne to marry the Duchess of Windsor, a hermaphrodite if I ever saw one.

Still, the royal family was red cheeked last month when the Prince denied any allegations as totally ludicrous. This is the man, after all, who wooed and won Lady Di. I remember when they first got married and watching one of the many TV movies about their courtship. She called him "Sir", which I have been trying to get my wife to call me ever since.

But he screwed that up, or maybe she just went nuts on him. From every-thing I've read it sounds like Lady Di got really flaked out there for a while. But maybe that's because she knew her husband was really pining away for Elton John.

Sure it's easy to laugh about the next King of England being a queen. I grew up reading about this putz my whole life because he is just a month older than me. I used to daydream what it would be like to be the Prince, and I have to admit it sure looked boring. Walking around with your hands behind your back, all the time. No pocket pool for this boy, no way.

It's gotta be rough these days for Charles. He marries well, dumps her and the world falls in love with her and then she is killed. Meanwhile you're dat-ing your first cousin's aunt, a hag with the smile of Secretariat. The world ridicules you, your sons probably hate you, and then some homo claims to have walked in on you in a compromising position with the guy who squirts the toothpaste on your brush.

My Christmas wish for Charles is a month vacation in Ireland where he can unwind and get away from the spotlight. A nice cottage to drink poteen in over the holidays. And if he gets lonely, a herd of sheep comes down the road every couple hours.

CHAPTER EIGHT

2004

COMPLAINT DEPT.

Irish American News
May 2004

Some guy wrote a letter to the editor last week complaining about me. He signed it, "sincerely, John McLaughlin."

Mr. McLaughlin was scolding editor Cliff Carlson for having columnists like myself, Tom Boyle, and Chris Fogarty writing in the Irish American News.

I can't speak for Tom or Chris but on behalf of myself I would to like to simply say to Mr. McLaughlin that if he doesn't like my column perhaps he would like to kiss my fat Irish ass.

Oh I know that sounds crude Mr. McLaughlin, but I must be honest with you, as much as you don't believe I am, I'm used to criticism. I've been hearing it from bicycle seat sniffers like yourself for years, but something in your rant really ticked me off. I'll get to that below, but first I'd like to point out that this paper is blessed with several strong personalities and thank God for that. It is after all, an Irish paper, and our people are known for passionate opinions. It's obvious our editor even welcomes differing viewpoints like yours because he did after all print your letter.

Your complaint regarding my column in particular cited a recent— "essay that included the words "poofery", "pansies" and "homo." Did the editorial staff ever stop to consider that this sort of bullying schoolyard talk might be insulting to your gay readers and their friends and families?"

Well Mr. McLaughlin, I would like to apologize for that, and if you or any members of your family are poofs, pansies, or homos I'm truly sorry.

The essay in question was a satire on Prince Charles of England and a little bullying on the schoolyard may have been just what that fop needed.

As an Irish American I think I can safely skewer the British royal family in an Irish paper without upsetting my audience, save for only a few lace-curtain flannel mouth phonies such as yourself.

As for gay readers, I'm happy for them and I'm sure they would agree with me that your sexual orientation is entirely your own business Mr. McLaughlin.

But the one sentence in your letter that has me steamed is this one: "Houlihan's tired South side shtick might pay the bills but its dishonest and mawkishly nostalgic."

Well now you've pissed me off Mr. McLaughlin. Tired? Sure it is, I'm 55 years old and tired of listening to self appointed culture critics who get off on fakers like Frank McCourt and Charlie Rose or PBS documentaries on the Chicago frickin' river.

Nostalgic? Well yeah I'm guilty of that. I happen to enjoy stories of a simpler time, also sometimes known as "history".

Pay the bills? Hah, I wish!

But dishonest? Never sir. I am nothing if not honest, as constant as the Northern star when smelling out a phony and I challenge you to present the facts of my "dishonesty." The style of my writing is the way I speak, every day, except for a proliferation of F words not printable in this paper. If you don't like that, then don't read it pal. That's a nice way of telling you to kiss my fat Irish ass once again. How's that for honesty?

Mr. McLaughlin, if you desire a politically correct publication featuring bland columnists devoid of personality then stick to reading your Tribune and your Anna Quindlen books and leave the Irish American News to the "honest" people in this community.

Bugger Off!

'LIL MARY CARNEY

Irish Amercan News
July 2004

The canonization of the Gipper last month kind of reminded me how much that guy owes a large part of his presidency to my wife.

Back when he was president I had a scheme to oust Reagan, and make my wife an international country and western superstar at the same time. If only she would have gone along with it.

It was the 80's. Mary and I had just had twins and we were trying to support ourselves in show business. But the policies of Ronald Reagan were not very friendly to us, i.e. the have-nots. It seemed to me everyday I would read in the paper of something Reagan had squashed that would have helped us out.

My little Mary was just a young lady then and I wrote a song for her to sing that I felt could have catapulted her to stardom. The title of the song was, "Return My Call, Mr. President".

It was a funny/sad ballad of how a mother of two and her unemployed husband were trying to make ends meet amidst Reaganomics.

I can't remember all the lyrics but I do remember it was terrific. "Return My Call Mister President" was the kind of song Patsy Cline would have made a million seller. I wanted my wife Mary to come up with an act, her pretty blonde curls, don a short Texas skirt with cowboy boots, and a cowboy hat and we would bill her as "Little Mary Carney".

In retrospect I should have just sold the song to Tanya Tucker, so at least somebody could make a buck with it. But I was young and foolish, and I thought I could talk my little darling Mary into talking with a twang, by way of upstate New York. I've learned of course since then. I can't talk little Mary into anything she doesn't want to do.

I imagined watching her from the audience at Madison Square Garden: The spotlights hit little Mary Carney and flash off the rhinestones on her cowboy hat as she slides her hands over the microphone and we hear the sound a of a phone ringing.

An operator answers and says, "Good Evening, the White House."

That's when little Mary Carney would ask to speak to President Reagan, and the music would come up behind her as she crooned her tail of woe of the unemployed husband and the two little hungry children at home. She'd break your heart with her story but the operator would only tell her President Reagan was not available, he was busy counting jellybeans or taking a nap or getting a spanking from Nancy.

Little Mary Carney would hang up the phone with a tear in her eye and that's when the band would really kick it in with the chorus, as she'd belt it out.
Return my call Mister President
By Now it must be ev—i—dent
We can't live this wa..............ay
And Ketchup ain't no vegetable......no wa ay!

The song would break the Billboard top 100 and work its way up to number one and go platinum. It would become a crossover hit that started in country, but because of its timely political statement broke through as a pop/rock hit as well. Little Mary Carney would become a huge star and they would discover she could act as well and the next thing you know little Mary would be starring on Broadway in a country western OTHELLO starring Charlie Pride and Mary Carney as Desdemona.

The song would so move the emotions of America to the plight of overweight, unemployed actors and their families that Reagan would be driven from office for his indifference to the poor. And I would spend the rest of my life living off the royalties of that song and little Mary Carney's Hollywood career. I had a lovely mansion in Nashville all picked out.

But no.......she wouldn't do it. "I can't do that, I don't sing that well," she told me. False modesty my dear.

As I watched them bury Reagan last month that was the thought that kept running through my head. What if? Yes America, Reagan's funeral was sadder than I thought it was going to be. I even shed a tear as I sang it one last time.

Return my call Mister President
By Now it must be ev—i—dent

We can't live this wa..............ay
And Ketchup ain't no vegetable......no wa ay!

DRIEHAUS THE OPTIMIST

Irish American News
September 2004

I had the pleasure of playing golf last month with my old pal Frankie Moran. I shot a 143, pretty decent score, if I was bowling. But I discovered that an optimistic attitude is more important than the score.

I don't play golf that often, but the idea of participating in a sport which involves driving a cart and drinking beers just naturally appeals to me. Golf is enjoyable if you don't take it too seriously and as you can see by my score, I didn't.

I even skipped two holes so I could concentrate on the wise cracks and stories Frankie and I exchanged with Richie Golz and Bob Snyder, the other half of our foursome.

Frankie and I got to talking about the old Ed Sullivan show. I had just returned from Lake Geneva where I attended a party hosted by billionaire philanthropist Richard Driehaus. It was truly one of the most amazing experiences of my life, other than my wedding night.

It was awfully nice of Driehaus to invite me and I brought my son Paddy along and we hobnobbed with the A-list. The nice thing about the party was that nobody acted like a snob. They couldn't. Everybody was too blown away by the lavishness of the estate and entertainment to get stuffy.

I heard rumors that Richard had spent two million bucks on the party. Can you imagine? Now I've been known to make a pretty good dent in anybody's open bar bill, but I was like a mosquito on the whale at this one.

I'm guessing he had at least five hundred people at this thing and huge tents, which offered a great Beatles band, and tons of food and drink for all. Paddy and I ran into Neil Hartigan and Vince Gavin and his sons and we had some laughs checking out the crowd early in the evening.

Driehaus must've had at least a hundred fifty gorgeous young women drifting through the party, each more spectacular than the next.

A couple of hot chix with Driehaus & Paddy Houlihan

Around ten o'clock our attention was drawn to this huge outdoor movie projection screen. It was like being at the old Hi-Way drive-in without cars and classier dates. On the screen was the opening of the latest Austin Powers movie, except that Austin Powers was being played by Richard Driehaus.

The screen froze and the real Driehaus was standing next to the 50-foot version of himself, who then said, "Hey Richard, great party!"

Driehaus then gestured to another part of his estate that was cloaked in drapery and unveiled before the assembled crowd was a life size replica of

Caesar's Palace in Vegas. Everybody walked a path to the Vegas area. On each side of the path were hundreds of dancing girls doing their Vegas type shing-a-ling.

We got up to the main dance floor of this palace, complete with replica Roman columns and statues, and Driehaus has a band performing on-stage surrounded by dozens more dancing girls. The band was The Four Tops. You heard me, sugar pie honey bun.

Now I could do ten pages on this party but my point is...well it was just great. Paddy and I looked at each other and the next day he said, "The whole thing was like a dream, I'm not even sure it happened."

Driehaus is not your typical rich guy either. He grew up in St. Margaret of Scotland parish, went to Ignatius and donates tons of dough to the nuns and never lost his Southside perspective.

But at the beginning of the evening he had a guy doing an Ed Sullivan impression who was hilarious. He introduced the Beatles and then would say stuff like, "Right here on our show, we're gonna have a guy come out and give a monkey an enema!"

So that's how Frankie Mo and I got to talking about Ed Sullivan while we golfed that day. And we were shooting the breeze about Senor Wences and his hand puppets and just what an all around great night of entertainment ol' Ed gave America every Sunday.

And then Frankie brought up the guys with the plates. Remember those guys? They were jugglers or whatever, but they would have these long skinny sticks and would be spinning about twenty plates at a time while this wacky music played, probably Flight of the Bumblebee.

Now who attempts an act like that unless they are optimistic it will work? And it just goes to show you how important an optimistic attitude can be to your work. If you believe in yourself, if you believe that you can keep those plates spinning, chances are pretty good that you will. It's just the power of optimism.

Richard Driehaus must be awfully optimistic about his future success if he can blow two million bucks on a party. With that kind of attitude I hope he makes trillions for the next fifty years.

I tried to explain the power of optimistic thinking to my lovely wife Mary right after my golf game with Frankie Mo. "You see honey it's just a question of being optimistic. Eventually we will win Lotto if we just believe it's possible. We must approach life as if the glass is always half full."

To which my bride responded, "You never left a glass half full in your life!"

HUGH HOYLE

Irish American News
November 2004

He knew how to make his wife happy.

Hugh Hoyle hadn't been to confession in years. Sure he went to mass every Sunday at Old St. Pat's. He made sure everybody saw him reading the epistle in his pinstriped suit. Hugh figured he wasn't that much of a sinner. He missed his Easter duty but that was about it. He was a pillar of his community, and the impure thoughts that had plagued him as a young man had thankfully vanished.

He was living his life as the perfect Irish Catholic; he was a Notre Dame grad, fine father and obedient husband. His dental practice put braces on every kid in the parish, which helped pay for his BMW and his home in Edison Park, which the Mexican gardeners kept in pristine shape.

Hugh's wife went by the name of Caitlin Corrigan Hoyle, the three-name handle that announced to people, "I'm a bitch."

She was a very important person in her own right. After all, she was national chairwoman of the Society for the Prevention of Johnny pushing Jimmy out of line.

Each holiday season the Hoyles sent out their Christmas cards, a color photo of the Hoyle kids, (Erin, Shannon, Tara, and little Hughie), as they stood amidst the snow with their skis in Switzerland. The children were precious, with rosy cheeks and blonde hair, and young Hugh sported a sweater with a reindeer on it. The card read Happy Holidays, because they didn't want to offend any Jewish people.

But Hugh was feeling pangs of guilt lately about the orthodontics he had performed on the Fagan triplets. The girls teeth were almost perfect and their dad would be hard pressed to pay the bill, but Hugh knew he could make their smiles more sincere with a twelve thousand dollar procedure that would help finance his family trip to the Vatican where Hugh would personally pickup a Papal blessing for the Hoyles.

Hugh didn't want to confess to just any priest. The only priest he would be comfortable with would have to be Father Arty Gridley.

Gridley had started out as a parish priest at St. Margaret Mary's but the archdiocese paid for his doctorate and he had gone on to write dozens of books, including a salacious series of novels, which disguised and detailed the sex lives of Irish Catholics he had met in the confessional booth at his old parish.

Father Gridley was known nationwide as a Catholic theologian who wrote a weekly column promoting liberal views in the Tribune. He made piles of dough and bought himself an estate in Lake Geneva where Domers would attend his special summer masses in their golf carts on the 13th hole.

He saw himself as a voice crying out in the wilderness for tolerance of homosexuality and abortion. He was always photographed in his roman collar with his treacley smile that seemed to say, "The pope just doesn't get it."

Father Gridley was on Nightline regularly commenting on the morals of America and was on a first name basis with Merv Griffin.

Hugh Hoyle decided that he would confess his tiny sin to none other than Arty Gridley.

It wasn't easy getting an appointment. Gridley would only agree to hear Hugh's confession after he made a hefty donation to the Priests Without Partners political action fund.

Finally the big day arrived and Hugh Hoyle drove downtown with butterflies in anticipation of meeting the pornographer priest.

Once they got Hugh's sin out of the way, (Gridley assured him it was for a good cause), they started chatting. Hugh really opened up with Arty and told him some old Notre Dame stories and even quoted some Latin from one of Gridley's book. "Semper ubi sub ubi", — always wear underwear.

Father Gridley started throwing out Latin phrases from the mass and Hugh Hoyle came right back at him. He was astounded at how much he remembered but then again Hughie in his youth had always been the top altar boy, just like Senator John Kerry.

Finally Gridley invited Hugh to join him for a drink at Kitty O'Shea's where they could discuss his penance. The two Irish Catholics spent the next few hours laughing and telling stories of priests from their past.

Father Gridley offered up several Irish toasts, "I wrote this for Eddie Rosewell's wake."

Hugh hadn't heard the story Artie told him about the priest from St. Bede's who stole a million bucks and was arrested in his car with a prostitute. Maybe it was the booze or the newfound friendship with Father Artie that caused Hugh to blurt out, "At least it wasn't an altar boy!"

Father Gridley was not pleased with this remark. He sat back in the snug and leveled Hugh Hoyle with a steely glare. "Perhaps we should get to your penance before I confer absolution." Uh oh.

When Hugh got home that night, Caitlin screamed at him. "Where have you been? The McGuires are coming for a dinner party and you're not even dressed, and ...oh no, have you been drinking?"

Hugh made his second confession of the day and the bitch cooled down when she learned he had been hobnobbing with the famous Father Gridley.

"Well, why didn't you invite him for dinner? What's wrong with you? Honestly, do I have to do everything around here?"

Hugh lied and told Caitlin Corrigan Hoyle that Father Artie was having dinner with Ted Kennedy that night and couldn't make it. But he reassured his darling that they would be seeing a lot more of Father Artie Gridley.

She said, "Oh, why is that?"

Hugh smiled weakly, "Father Gridley needs quite a bit of dental work, gum surgery, and new dentures. I'm donating it."

That night Caitlin let Hugh work the TV remote for almost a full hour.

FRANKIE MORAN IN VEGAS

Irish American News
December 2004

"Money doesn't talk in Vegas, it screams out loud."

Frankie Moran uttered these words of wisdom to me as we sat at the bar in the Bellagio playing video blackjack in Las Vegas.

Frankie's money wasn't talking or screaming that night. It was sobbing.

Two weeks earlier I had received a call from my pals at the Brick Marketing Council and they asked me, "Hey we got a free trip for two to Vegas from radio station WZZN, the Zone. It's all expenses paid, you wanna go?"

The Pope's a Catholic, a bear poops in the woods, and I'm goin' to Vegas!

Of course I called my wife, the lovely Mary, and asked her if she would like to join me. "Absolutely not, that's the capital of all that is evil. That would be like going to hell!"

I was counting on that answer.

Well I'll just go with a buddy. My old pal Frankie Moran the fireman was available and a junket to Vegas with him would be like hanging out with a combination of Shecky Greene and Hal Roche.

We left on a Wednesday night and returned Saturday night. One more night there and I would be writing this from the nut house. The little sleep we got was punctuated by the sound of Mo doing his B-52 impression as he snored and prayed to Our Lady of Keno.

The day of our departure I received some sad news from my pal Willie West, via his brother Ray. Maybe you heard about it. They informed me of the sad passing last week of Roland, "Larry", LePrise, at 83 of natural causes. Larry LePrise wrote the lyrics to "The Hokey Pokey" and his family had been deeply grieved by his demise. It wasn't the death so much as the selection of a comfortable coffin for Larry's burial. The mortified family was present when the undertaker put his left leg in, ...and then all holy hell broke loose.

Armed with this joke and not enough cash we hit Vegas.

Among the highlights were the free massage, manicure, and pedicure thrown in from "the Zone".

Frankie and I sat next to each other as the girls bathed our feet after the massage. "I guess I'm officially a metrosexual." Rodney Dangerfield in a robe crackin' up the pedicurists.

We stayed at the Hard Rock hotel with a group of blue haired punk rocker fans of a musical group called Korn. Groupies, basically who had paid for the pleasure of being in Korn's presence.

Are you guys gonna go see Korn?

"We've seen it, and not in the best places either."

Frankie and I hit the casinos and sports book rooms of the Mirage, MGM Grand, Caesar's Palace, and when we weren't gambling we people watched in the Indigo Lounge of Bally's. We switched to screwdrivers the second day because we knew the Vitamin C would be beneficial during our expedition to Sin City.

Sully's bar in Bally's is named for Bill Sullivan, the longtime casino host. Sully comped us tickets to the Vegas showgirl revue playing at Bally's, "Jubilee". The show triggered a laughing fit that went on for the next two days.

"Jubilee" was your standard Vegas revue; it's been running for thirty some years. The dancing girls were scantily clad of course, but the dancing boys in the show really stood out. These guys made Liberace look like John Wayne. And they're singing and dancing in tuxedos about "when a guy meets a girl", yeah right.

The next number features these two little Chinese guys, twins. They've got this dancing contortionist act, sort of like Mummenshcanz. And they're smiling their asses off as they both squeeze into either end of a Chinese handcuffs type tube. Frankie turns to me and says, "I'll bet these guys know the hokey-pokey."

And that's when all holy hell broke loose.

A Roman centurion bit followed the Chinese contortionists number and all these guys come dancing out wearing just a leather jockstrap with metal studs on it. And they're shaking their fannies all over the place and Frankie and I are now convulsed with laughter. The girls and boys are dancing around and the general of the centurions' steps forward in his jockstrap to sing.

You can tell he's the general because he's the only one who wears a pillbox type hat on his head. I guess that's what Roman centurions wore in those days, a leather jock, a belt, and Jackie Kennedy's hat.

I turned to Frankie and said, "Any minute now they're gonna do a Mandingo number."

Sure enough they start singing the intro to Samson and Delilah, and Samson dances out in his loincloth, looking like a gay Dr. J. Frankie shouts "Mandingo!" and then we had to leave. Our laughter had begun to disrupt the show.

The rest of the audience was enthralled by this hokey pokey. Half the cast was doing the hokey onstage and the other half was doing the pokey backstage.

We exited the theater and propelled our way across the strip, bouncing around casinos, droppin' dough, and working the hokey pokey joke into almost every conversation with the hustlers, sharks, and oddball characters in Vegas.

At one point, Frankie gazed out over the hordes of humanity walking the carpets and said, "I can't believe that there's this many people in the world that I don't know."

They know us now Frankie, thanks to the late, great Larry LePrise.

CHAPTER NINE

2005

PONTIAC POLITICIAN PUTZ

Irish American News
January 2005

I recently celebrated a birthday. It was no big deal. Went out for dinner with my family late that evening, had a couple Mannies, and hit the sack. But the daydreaming on your birthday can be terrific.

You think of all the things you could or should do to celebrate, to pamper yourself, to excuse yourself from your ordinary humdrum routine. How many times have news anchors told their shocked audience, "The naked man who police eventually overpowered and arrested was celebrating his birthday."

And you shout back at the TV, "Well of course, that's why they call it a birthday suit!"

Yes, I'll admit to staring out the window on my birthday and fantasizing about running across Michigan avenue buck naked and cavorting in front of the Millennium Park fountain. Although it was pretty darn cold that day and the shrinkage factor would be extreme. Combined with being an Irishman, the Arctic air would have neutered this nudist.

If the cops came I would just freeze into position and pretend Italy had sent a copy of Michelangelo's David to the new park. Yeah, looks like ol' Dave gained an extra hundred pounds and grew some back hair, among other things, on the journey over from Florence.

Nah, I guess I've passed the age of birthday streaking. The image of me naked on a December morn might garner me an arrest for indecent exposure but it's more likely I would be charged with some terrorist act. The sight of my birthday butt could cause some real damage to the population, so I'll keep it under wraps for another year.

By the time I'm eighty, well maybe I'll unveil the old bones then. What could the authorities do to me at that point?

I got an email that same day from a politician wishing me a happy birthday. I wondered how this guy knew it was my birthday. We had never met and I wasn't a constituent. So I emailed him back and said, basically, "Who the hell are you? A state senator from Pontiac, Illinois, and why do you know when my birthday is? And why do you care?"

The senator must have an awful lot of time on his hands because I got a reply from him about five minutes later. He said he got my birthday from voter registration records and had me in his files for sending news about Springfield legislation. "I didn't mean to offend you."

It's pretty obvious this guy will run for higher office. He probably has some mopey kid who sends out these emails to Illinois voters on their birthday, your tax dollars at work.

But it gave me an idea, since Senator Dan Rutherford is so interested in my happiness on my birthday, and every other day I'm sure. Maybe Senator Rutherford could introduce a bill in the state legislature granting amnesty for anyone arrested nude on his or her birthday. Especially in his hometown of Pontiac.

Of course my birthday meant I was another year older and it gave me pause. I asked my sons if I'm getting grumpier as I get older and they told me, "Yes!"

I had a feeling that was happening to me, because right after my birthday I was doing some Christmas shopping at Marshall Fields. I bought some shirts for my boys and complained about the price as I handed them to the cashier. Then I asked her for gift boxes, which she provided. Then I said, "Why don't you have any chairs in this joint for somebody to sit down?"

She went out of her way to be nice and showed me a chair around the corner and told me to relax while she put my gifts in boxes. Then she came back and presented them to me. "Would you like to open the box and see how nice they look? Would you like me to open the box for you?" Uh, okay, sure, sure.

Then I got off my tired old butt and walked to the counter to ask for bags for each present. She handed me my packages and said, "Would you like me to accompany you to guest services where we can have you call a member of your family to come and pick you up and take you home?"

Was she messin' with me? I looked at the clerk, her name tag said Kim. She just smiled back at me. I told her that wouldn't be necessary, just point me towards the down escalator. She said, "I'll walk you over there."

Now of course I felt like I was a hundred year old grumpy old man and she was humoring me to get rid of the old fart. I can't blame her I guess. I wouldn't have been so grumpy had I taken the opportunity on my birthday to run naked through Pontiac, Illinois.

Eureka! That's the solution to grumpy old folks everywhere. Let them run around naked on every birthday after the age of 55. So what do you think of that legislation, Senator Dan? Could you get behind it?

FATHER MAC

Irish American News
February 2005

Phony priests get under my skin. They wear the roman collar like a crown upon their head. But last month we lost an original, a priest who wore humility like a jock wears his jersey.

Monsignor Ignatius McDermott has a front row seat in Heaven today, right on the fifty-yard line. It's exactly where he always wanted to be.

When my mom died about ten years ago, Iggy came to her wake. I shook his hand and he had this huge grin on his face as he said to me, "Mike, your mom's got a front row seat tonight!"

His comment made me feel great because if anybody knew at that moment where my mother was, it would have been Father Mac. I'd watched him in action over the years and I knew if anybody had a pipeline to Jesus it was Iggy McDermott.

Pete Nolan first introduced me to Father Mac about twenty years ago. We were just starting a television production business together and Pete had the idea that our first project should be a pro bono production of a fundraising video for Father Mac. We figured our biz would be blessed if we donated the first one to the "pastor of skid row."

Father Mac was working with the winos and bust-outs on Madison Street in those days, doing what Jesus would have done.

He was one of the first to recognize alcoholism as a disease and not a character flaw. He had started Haymarket House, an alcoholic treatment center and shelter for the lost souls who trudged from bottle to bottle trying to climb out of the gutter. He offered a warm bed, food, friendship and detox.

Father Mac's dream then was a large operation in the west Madison neighborhood that would provide medical and psychological care for a much larger group of forgotten folks. It would be called The McDermott Center, and it stands today on west Washington as a testament to the work of Iggy McDermott.

Pete and I met with Father Mac one afternoon to pitch him on the video idea. The late, great Mike Howlett joined us that day and told us he would find a way to get the cash to pay for the camera crews and editing. Howlett picked up the phone and called Ed Duffy over at the state department of alcohol and substance abuse. Duffy got us the dough as soon as he heard the idea. Father Mac's name worked miracles.

The star of the video was a guy who Father Mac had helped some 30 years before and who had gone on to become a successful businessman. We put him on camera and he told of his days as a young alkie living in a flophouse until he met Father Mac. He spoke of the serenity that came over him after that meeting and how he quit the booze and turned his life around. Then he donated fifty grand to Father Mac and his dream of McDermott Center. It was an amazing testimonial and we captured it on tape.

But the best part of our production was walking with Father Mac on his rounds as he met the guys on the street. We went to a soup kitchen and Father Mac handed out Winstons to the winos. He didn't lay any bible on them and spoke to them as if they were celebrities. He wanted them to feel good about themselves and it worked.

After Pete and I finished the video project Father Mac became our family friend. He visited my dad when he was dying and came to all my shows and sent me cards on every holiday, especially St. Patrick's Day. I'll bet he sent out thousands of those cards.

Father Mac was like an old coach you could always go back and talk to and know he would understand your problems and put in a word with the big guy for you. Ask him to say a prayer for you and he would make it a home run.

The moment of the video I'll never forget was a shot of three guys with Father Mac telling their stories. One of the men had obviously seen some rough days, his face was scarred and he was missing an eye. As he spoke of his relationship with Father Mac he choked up, "Dis guy is da best friend I ever had in my life." As the old rummy said those words, a tear somehow formed in his empty eye socket and trickled down his craggy face.

Chicago sheds that tear today as Father Mac joins his pal Jesus. It's not Iggy we are crying about but ourselves because we will never see his like again. He's got a front row seat tonight.

GABRIEL UNDER THE BRIDGE

Irish American News
April 2005

"Looks like there's somebody living under this bridge!", whispered Mike "Oats" McNeal as he gave me the high sign and pointed over the side. We were roaming around the river just south of Cermak.

We discovered a hood of the homeless while doing research for a film we're working on, "Tapioca".

I leaned over the side of the bridge and gazed down, and there was a man looking up in apprehension, smiling.

It was the last Thursday in January, temperature twelve degrees and Oats and I were freezing our cookies off. Our new friend didn't look like he was cold, but he also didn't look like he wanted a visit from "the man". I flashed a phony badge and told him we wanted to come down and see his home. The guy didn't want any trouble, and he didn't seem to speak English.

Oats handed me a finnski and said, "Show him this."

Cash money beats a fake badge any day. The guy nodded when I said, "We're coming down there to see you."

We walked back across the bridge and down the adjacent street to a fenced area along the river. The gate was padlocked with a chain but you could see there was plenty of room to squeeze through. Two stray dogs trotted around in the snow at the entrance where the man had left his shopping cart parked. I said to Oats, "Maybe I should get a baseball bat out of the trunk for these dogs."

"Nah, they'll be okay."

You don't think they have rabies or anything? They might take a bite out of my crotch.

"Nah, look at 'em, they're not dangerous."

Well in that case, you can go first.

"Nooooo I don't think so."

I spoke to the dogs while I squeezed through the fence gate, "Don't you guys bite me now."

They sniffed me over pretty good and then Oats got the same treatment. We told the dogs we just wanted to meet their master and see his home. As we walked around the riverbank towards the bridge, another man mysteriously appeared out of nowhere.

I heard Oats mutter from behind me, "Where'd he come from?"

The first guy met us halfway on the snowy path. He had his hands in his pockets as if holding a weapon. I gave him the old Dave Garroway salute and said, "Peace".

Oats said, "That's right, we come in peace."

We introduced ourselves.

What's your name?

"Gabriel."

We shook hands, and Gabe gestured to the path towards his crib. I asked Gabe to lead the way, mainly because I didn't want to turn my back on this guy. He didn't look cold because he was under anesthesia. Gabe's breath was 900 proof. If you lit a match he could have blown up the bridge.

We walked to the riverbank and met the other fella. Mexican guy says his name is Jose. That's as bad as two Irish guys both named Mike.

How long have you been out here under the bridge, Gabe?

Two months.

That would be December and January of this very brutal winter. Jose nixes his photo op but Gabe is very agreeable and poses in front of the blanket that frames his crib. He pulls it back to reveal an inner blanket decorated with the Flintstones. Cool, they lived in a cave too.

I asked Oats, "Think we should go in?"

"If we go in, we may never come out. We could wind up as dinner."

Gabe pulled back the Flintstones curtain for a photo. Inside was a small red milk crate with a radio on top of it. Gabriel's quarters were immaculate, as if they had vacuumed. Tied to the wire fence outside his front door was a shard of mirror about the size of a big pizza slice. It struck me funny at first. Then I was humbled by it. In the midst of this penury, this ultimate tapioca, Gabe retained dignity.

We thanked the men and laid some bread on Gabe, enough for more of that heating fuel he and Jose imbibed. I wanted to say more but we couldn't understand each other.

Or could we? I took a final look at Gabe. He had an aura about him and I started thinking about the archangel Gabriel, the guardian of paradise.

Gabriel

Gabriel is the highest-ranking angel of Christian, Hebrew, and Muslim religions. He is the angel of the annunciation of the Madonna; the resurrection of Christ; mercy, vengeance, death, and revelation. According to the Old Testament he was in on the destruction of Sodom and Gomorrah, the massacre of the Assyrian army, the wrestling episode with Jacob, and the burial of Moses. The bible says Gabriel will appear on the last day and blow the final trumpet calling all living and dead to face the final judgment of God. Gabriel has been known to descend to earth to inform and inspire the faithful. He is the Lord's messenger.

Gabriel—living under a Chicago bridge behind a Flintstones blanket.

As good a spot as any for some trumpet practice.

DA POPE

Irish American News
May 2005

"If you wanna make some money in this world, you should start your own religion."

Sometimes I regret not following that sage advice my dad gave me when I was in my early twenties. Instead I went into show business and have been struggling with various degrees of tapicoa ever since.

I had doubts then about the credibility of the "Church of Houli". But since then I've watched idiots like Jimmy Swaggart, Bennie Hinn, and Pat Robertson as they scrunch up their foreheads on TV and pretend to pray and take in the suckers cash. Man I could do that, probably better than they do.

But alas, I was baptized a Catholic and that's the jacket I will wear until the day I meet Elvis in heaven.

Some folks got pooped from all the papal pomp over the last several weeks, but not me. The Pope was my hero.

The lovely Mary and I were lucky enough to attend the Pope's Yankee Stadium mass in Gotham in 1979. She was pregnant with the boys then, so they can say they were there too. It was electrifying just being in his presence. Earlier in the day we had stood along the street outside the United Nations when he drove by and I yelled out, "Papa!"

John Paul made it cool to be Polish and I admired his hard line politics. He was a pope with incredible balls. I guess that was it, his courage in the face of so many adversities. Karol Wojtyla was also an actor and playwright. We ain't all bums.

In the Vatican there is supposedly a room down the hall from the conclave and that room is called "the room of tears". Upon election as Pope you must walk alone to that room and enter. Once inside the "room of tears" the full weight of the responsibility hits the new Pope, hence the name.

A new Pope will slowly close the door behind him after entering the "room of tears" and he hears the scratchy old Brooklyn accented voice of Morrie, the Jewish tailor to the Pope, as he approaches with tape measure draped around his neck. "Ya look like a 46-portly, Your Holiness, lemme fix ya right up with some vestments."

The Pope is then measured for a complete set of Papal sportswear by Morrie as he shouts down the basement, "Hey Sol, I'm gonna need a 6 and 3/8 beanie, and get it up here pronto!"

It could happen.

By the time you read this we'll probably have a new Pope. Who will it be?

I'm thinkin' it's about time we had an Irish Pope, someone who looks like me. I can see him now, Pope Mickey.

Upon his election he will appear at the window in St. Peter's square with a big smile on his face as he speaks to the world in his brilliant brogue, "How are ye, I'm the pope, -yes I'm the pope and there's gonna be a few changes made around here now that I'm the pope. We're goin' back to fish on Fridays!

We're gonna do away with the water and wine at mass and from now on it's gonna be whiskey and water!"

The pope comes to Chicago and gets pulled over on the Ike for drinking and driving.

"Do ya have any idea who ya just pulled over officer? I'm the pope. Just because I'm driving a Chevy Lumina, don't mean I ain't the Pope. Now I'll admit I've had a bit to drink but I've just come from concelebrating a great big thingamajig mass at Grants Park. Beejazus, it was better than taste of Chicago.

Now you just put that Breathalyzer away young fella, I'm sure we can work this out, Officer Murphy is it? I bet your old mother was a saint.... well I can make it official.

Sure you just forget about this whole thing and first thing tomorrow morning I'm going' to have your old mum canonized. Sure her first miracle will be getting me outta this DUI!"

An Irish Pope, it's certainly worth praying for.

News Flash—As this paper went to press Cardinal Ratzinger of Germany was named Pope Benedict XVI. The new Pope has a reputation for being a conservative hard liner. He may not be Irish but he will drive the goo-goos nuts and that is good enough for me to say, "Viva il Papa!"

JOHN HOULIHAN

Irish American News
June 2005

Death was working overtime among my friends last April. Every time I turned around, another pal was croaking. It got so bad for a while there that my pal Jackie Casto said, "I was afraid to answer the phone!"

The grim reaper started calling on people close to me, like Sean Farrell of the Fighting Farrells in Beverly. It was a sad wake, kid was only 21. I saw Casto in the funeral home and he told me he was heading over to Mrs. Rundle's wake, where her son Rick was entertaining the mourners at Donellan's between quick trips across Western Avenue to Ken's.

And then I heard about Mike Carney buying the farm, Westside Jim's brother. And somebody told me they had found Nancy the bartender from Ken's passed away in her sleep on another morning. And Jackie's cousin Tony Casto had a heart attack and kicked the bucket.

And then my brother John died. That's when it stares you right in the face. Johnny stared right back and laughed.

When it looked like he was going to be checking out he told me, "I'm not afraid of death."

I said, "Yeah, you'll get to see mom and dad."

John said, "Yeah, and James Dean."

John was nicknamed "Bobo" by his pals in high school. He eschewed the name later in life but it was the perfect handle for the tall, gangly Irish kid with the wise-ass grin. John was the fourth of us seven kids, the middle-man, and the negotiator between the older and younger factions in our family.

His reputation as a hooligan in his youth was earned with a subversive wit that loved to spar with authority figures.

Sister Rosary had released the entire school early one afternoon at Christ the King grammar school to hunt for John and his eighth grade pals who had ditched that day. It was the largest manhunt in Beverly history.

My mom used to love to tell the story of the day she was waiting for a pre-scription at Waxman's drugstore. Louie Waxman had said, "I'll be right with you Mrs. Houlihan." And the lady next in line said, "Houlihan? Are you John Houlihan's mother?" My mom beamed, "Why yes, yes I am."

"Well he's a terrible boy!"

My mom thought that was hilarious, and told the lady, "Well you don't know him like I do."

He got kicked out of Leo high school in his sophomore year and my old man sent him to a boarding school hoping it would straighten the lad out. The headmasters had pledged to whip him into shape at Bullis Academy in Washington D.C., where "Spartan simplicity is a way of life."

The rest of us kids were thrilled when he busted out a few months later. Bobo Houlihan had been expelled from Bullis Academy. The headmaster said John was, "a detrimental influence to the rest of the student body."

While off-campus one night, John's rebellious spirit inspired him to punch a horse, while a policeman was riding it.

He went to college and served in the army as a psychological warfare expert and editor of the Special Forces newspaper, Veritas.

As a young adult he found avenues for his irreverent humor as editor of a series of tabloid newspapers with headlines like "Gophers Ate My Baby!"

His old pal Jack Sullivan was courting his wife Mary in those days and they frequented the Irish dances all over Chicago. Jack said, "I never ditched him on a weekend. If he didn't have a date we'd bring him along."

Mary was from the old country and still laughs about John doing his own booze-fueled version of Riverdance while the greenhorns fumed.

John opened a bar in Milwaukee, "Mike Houlihan's" and was sued by the restaurant chain "Houlihan's". John counter-sued and defended our family name when he pointed out that the chain was a corporate fake and there wasn't one actual Houlihan with any ties to the restaurants. "The name means a lot more to me than your recipe for creamy salad dressings and cheeseburgers."

Johnny met his wife Vicky in the north woods of Wisconsin. He realized every South-sider's fantasy, marrying a gorgeous girl whose father owned a liquor store. Vicky's dad hired John to run the business and he became a solid citizen in Milwaukee, where he and Vicky raised their kids, Jonathan and Kerry.

In his forties John contracted MS. The disease may have trapped his body for the next twenty years but his mind was still a fertile playground for his wacky humor. We'd talk on the phone every week and Johnny would have me crying with laughter with his stories of weirdoes in Wisconsin.

My brother Willie and I visited him right before he died. John was on morphine and somewhat incoherent. We didn't know what the hell he was talking about when he laughed and told us, "The VA hospital is givin' me an Irish orchestra!"

Now he's in heaven. I've been around the block and I've met some fascinating people, but my brother John was the funniest man I ever knew. That Irish orchestra is playing his symphony now.

TREE-HUGGER

Irish American News
July 2005

Last Friday night I went to the Sox game. They won of course, and it was great being among a large group of Southsiders who got increasingly vocal as the innings flew by. By the eighth inning they've shut off the beer and the boozers finally turn their focus to the diamond. Boos are shouted out as much as attaboys.

I was in good company, with my sons Bill and Paddy. We joined the ticket sellers over by aisle 116. The White Sox ticket sellers are a cool crew, and we had many laughs and then watched the Sox win in another thrilling finale. It was sweet.

Saturday morning, I'm laying in bed dreaming of the 1959 Go-Go White Sox. Ted Kluszewski was my hero. He was a big tree.

So I'm laying in bed muttering, "the big tree, the big tree." The lovely Mary says, "What about the big tree?"

And then I hear these guys in trucks outside my window, and I hear the Mexican guys jabberin' and the boss yells, "We're gonna cut down this big tree."

I look out the window and there are ten landscape guys and a huge truck with a crane and a gigantic wood chipper. I grab my shorts and run out the door; "Hey what the hell do you guys think you're doing?"

The guy says, "We got to cut down this tree, it's got Dutch Elm disease."

It was the largest tree on my property. Well, actually the property of the Village. But it was this gigantic tree that went about sixty feet into the air like a benevolent Colossus. The tree cast shade for a hundred yards in all directions. I used to tell Mary, "If lightning ever strikes that tree and it falls on our house, we are toast!"

Oh, how I wish I could take back those words. My tree! The men had come to cut down my tree, without warning, in the early hours of a weekend, when they knew I'd be at my most vulnerable.

I thought of how Ted "Big Klu" Kluszewski would have handled the situation and flexed my muscles while throwing the F word about liberally. The tree guy looked at me like he had seen this act a million times.

The "branch manager" says I should call the department of public works. I run inside the house and grab the phone, nobody answers on Saturday, of course. So I hang up and call the Mayor. "Save my tree!"

I look at the clock, it's 7:45 AM on a Saturday and I'm calling' the Mayor. Am I nuts?

The voice mail gives out his cell phone number, and I call it. It's a pager and I punch in my number. Then I called the cops!

I run back outside to hug my tree and the tree guy says, "Who'd you call?"

I called the mayor.

"I figured it would be something like that."

You're flippin' a' right it's something like that, I love that tree!

The cops show up, River Forest's finest. They showed compassion and the tree guy finally said, "Well your tree is gonna live another day, we'll come back next week." I guess so I could get used to the idea.

So I'm lying on the couch later that day, watching the Sox win on TV. The phone rings and it's the Mayor. Uh oh.

The Mayor says he's right outside my house, why don't I come out and talk to him. I hustle out the back door and there is the Mayor of River Forest, Frank Paris. I explain my early morning call and apologize for disturbing him that Saturday morning. He says, "I was on the golf course at 7:45, you didn't wake me up."

Frank Paris has the Wisdom of Solomon. We walk over to my tree to say our good-byes. Like a bereavement counselor he talks me through the reasons the tree must go. Mayor Frank told me they would plant two fast growing trees on the parkway to take the place of the mighty Elm.

If I was Ted Kluszewski, he had become Sox manager Al Lopez and coached me about my sacrifice play. I know that "only God can make a tree", but I also know that only the great village of River Forest could elect a mayor with the prudence and understanding of Frank Paris. If my tree must die to save the lives of other trees on our block, then 'tis a noble thing.

My tree

I stared up at the tree. It didn't look sick. The tree was still mighty and magisterial, the wind ruffling her mane. I thought of how that tree had stood sentry over our house for probably the last fifty years, through generations of owners. There had been a lot of desire under that elm.

As I walked back inside I said a silent prayer that wood from my tree could be used to make a White Sox bat and lead them to the World Series this year. It could happen! I sure hope Frank Paris is a Sox fan.

WHERE'S MY LIMO?

Irish American News
September 2005

"Vulgar" should have been Leo Shull's middle name. Shull was my boss in the late seventies in New York, right after I got married. He was the editor and publisher of "Show Business" newspaper, a weekly rag that ran audition notices and a "must read" for poor saps like me who trudged the boulevard of Broadway.

I met Shull on my wedding night in the Edwardian Room of the Plaza hotel where I danced with my wife. I walked over and introduced myself to this ogre, hoping for some publicity on my nuptials. I told Leo I had just wed the best looking babe in show biz and my career was ready to explode. Eighteen months later I was his chauffeur.

Shull owned a '77 Cadillac, he didn't have the dough for a limo. But he was paying me to wear my doubled-breasted, navy blue blazer and drive him and his old lady around Gotham. He gave me a hat too, which I only wore when the Shulls were in the back seat. He encouraged me to speak with phony foreign accents, which I declined. Shull kvetched, "Come on, I thought you said you were an actor!"

You ain't payin' me enough for that. That shut him up. Leo was always late with the dough re mi.

It was a demeaning job for a man of my stature, but I figured I might make some valuable show biz connections while chauffeuring the Shulls.

I'd sit in bistros with fellow thespians and tell them I was working for "Show Business" newspaper. Might as well have told them I was driving David Berkowitz around. The elite poor loathed Shull.

But I admired his chutzpah; the guy had put together his tiny empire from selling mimeographed audition notices to actors on the street for nickels. He was a natural born hustler.

He looked like Mr. Potter from It's a Wonderful Life, his cummerbund ready to pop and wore a constant expression of somebody who has just discovered they have food poisoning.

After I dropped Shull and his spouse at the Opera, I would toss the hat in the back and cruise around Manhattan in his Cadillac. I felt like an imposter at first, a punk kid driving a Caddy, but the music from the radio would dispel any notion of the fact that I didn't belong on Broadway in another man's Caddy. The hours I spent cruising in Shull's Deville more than made up for the torture of listening to that putz gripe about all the shmucks he had seen at the show.

On Saturdays I would drive Shull's wife, Clare, out to Long Island with her girlfriend to visit her mother in the nursing home. We always stopped at Loehman's, where the ladies would do some shopping on the way. I'd smile to myself as I listened to Clare dish Leo to her pal. The old gals seemed to like me, and even took me to lunch once...at McDonalds.

After dropping the ladies off at the home I'd hit Rockaway Beach Boulevard and quaff beers while watching the football game. I'd park the Caddy right in front of the bar window and BS with the boys. I'd point to the car and ask the guys, "Have you seen my new Caddy? Yeah, it's a sweet ride."

26 years later I'm sittin' at the bar in Kevil's talkin' to a couple of Suzies-Hosty and Kunkel. I pointed out the window and told the girls, "Have you seen my new Caddy? Yeah, it's a sweet ride!"

That's right; I'm now the proud owner of a 2002 cashmere sedan Deville with white ragtop and white wall tires. It looks like a glass of champagne, fully loaded, grey leather interior with only 36,000 miles on her. The previous owner was an Irish priest in St. Louis. Could she be any cleaner?

I don't feel like an imposter anymore as I tool around in my Caddy. Now I'm the Monsignor on his way to a tee time at Beverly. I'm Biggy Smalls before he bought it. I'm Elvis in my dusty gold caddy.

I parked the Caddy in my driveway the day I brought it home and honked the horn for my wife to come out and feast her eyes.

"How do you like my new Caddy?"

"It's vulgar!"

Leo Shull would have been proud. It's a sweet ride.

Me & my caddy

MARY'S BIG BREAK

Irish American News
October 2005

My poor wife, I married the hell out of her.

She was a star of stage and screen when we got hitched. But she eschewed the world of show biz to become the mother of the infamous Houlihan brothers, Bill and Paddy. That hasn't been an easy road, looking after the men in her life. And to top it off she's been living on the brink of financial ruin for the last 27 years because she chose a husband who is more interested in eating the bread than winning it.

Through the years her qualities of beauty and grace have only intensified, tempered no doubt with a great sense of humor. Living in our house with three wild men, you hang onto the only things that will keep you sane. Her laughter and faith have preserved her through the maelstrom.

In addition to being able to look at the funny side of her family's failings, she finds solace in prayer. Over the years the lovely Mary has even become somewhat of a theologian. She works the beads on a daily basis and can cite chapter and verse on the history of the Vatican. That's why her recent adventure as an actress made us all laugh.

Mary got an audition call last week from an agent for a photo print job. I listened to the voice mail from her agent mentioning the fact that the job could be worth $2500 and urged her to make a comeback.

She put her best face forward and went to the photographer's studio for a "look-see", where they snap photos and then decide if you are chosen for the advertisement.

I was excited for her and also was mentally counting that 25 hundred bucks when I left that morning for Sheriff Mike Sheahan's golf outing. It was a beautiful day at Gleneagles with over 800 supporters of the Sheriff strutting their stuff. I felt like I was at a McGaffers convention.

I got home that night and there was my sweet little darling at the kitchen table. I asked her, "How did the audition go?" She smiled.

The photographer had asked her for a couple poses, "Give me American Gothic" and then, "Now love is in the air." I'm sure she was brilliant and the photographer thought so too as he told her they would let her know.

Mary asked the guy, "What is the product for this advertisement?"

He hemmed and hawed, "It's a pharmaceutical product."

What kind of pharmaceutical product?

"Caverject."

What is Caverject used for?

"Erectile dysfunction."

Now this was particularly amusing to myself, the boys, and even Mary, as we imagined the reaction of the ladies in her prayer group if they saw her delicate beauty in "before and after" photos, hawking a drug for droopy danglers.

Mary's modesty forbade this enterprise and she told the photographer she wouldn't be interested in the job. I was relieved as well because I certainly didn't want friends looking at ads of "Houli's wife" promoting this wonder drug.

I was even more amused when I checked out Caverject on the Internet. It's not your standard pill for potency, but must be administered by injecting your willy with a hypodermic syringe. I doubt if this product is going to take off. Who is so desperate they would resort to a needle for some nookie?

I was also shocked to read some of the potential side effects of this drug. I'm not making this up, "The most common side effect is mild to moderate pain in the penis during and/or after injection, reported by about one-third of users. A small amount of bleeding may occur at the injection site. As with any injection, the site can become infected. Call your doctor if you notice any redness, lumps, swelling, tenderness, or curving of the erect penis."

And if your scrotum explodes, discontinue use of Caverject.

I don't envy the advertising guys who were assigned this account. But they won't have the lovely Mary Carney modeling for their elixir. She's mine.

The Caverject incident has been a source of many laughs around our house lately, and Mary laughs too. She has a terrific sense of humor. She can take the needling.

CHAPTER TEN

2006

THE OTTO CHRONICLES

Irish American News
January 2006

Otto had been in the nuthouse for ten years, but we thought he might be faking.

Maybe he figured it was three squares a day, read the paper, unlimited napping, a roof over your head and nobody bothers you. Knowing Otto, I'm sure he developed his own philosophy on his stay at the nursing home.

Otto had been bullshittng us since we were in first grade, so his diagnosis a decade ago didn't really surprise anybody. Technically it was called alcohol encephalopoly, a fancy shmancy way of sayin' Otto had suffered brain damage from Mr. Booze. When we first went out to visit him at the home, I talked to his brother who told me, "He suffers from delusions. He thinks he served in Viet Nam and has grandiose conspiracy assignments for the CIA."

That was the same type of malarkey Otto had been spinning to us as kids hanging out at the b-ball courts in Beverly. Otto was well read and had a keen intellect, which he used to great effect as a provocateur and troublemaker in his youth. He had a caustic wit that he began fueling with beer in seventh grade.

We admired him, not for his falsehoods, but his dedication to the detail of his devilish designs. Otto was a master who weaved his BS into a rich tapestry of eccentric lies. My old pal Malachy Keane had grown up next door to Otto. It was Malachy who initiated our first sojourn to visit Otto at the nursing home, three years into his institutialization.

Otto started right in with his delusions once we sat down in the cafeteria for a cup of coffee and got comfortable with our old friend. He appeared normal, even looked like he had gained weight, but he let it drop in the midst of our bonhomie that he had just flown in the night before from a mission in Nicaragua.

We actually went along with it, rather than challenge his fantasy and potentially set him off on a psychotic episode. We always knew he was crazy, but now it was official and we had some reverence for his lunacy.

After twenty minutes into our banal reminiscing, I gave Malachy the high sign that we should split. Otto walked us to the front door as we said adios. Standing in front of the Waukegan nursing home with its lovely view of the parking lot, Malachy remarked to Otto "This seems like a nice place."

Otto mumbled, "Yeah, it's not bad, for Kansas."

Malachy eyes bugged as he whispered to me, "He thinks we're in Kansas!"

It was just enough oddball logic that convinced us then that maybe the doctors we're right. This guy had burned out several spark plugs.

Malachy and I left that day of our first visit and drove directly to a bar. We felt bad for our old pal, but it seemed pretty apparent that he was not coming back from whatever planet he was now operating. That was about seven years ago.

Malachy called me last week and told me he was flying in from Austin and would I be interested in paying Otto another visit? Mack said, "It will be a corporal work of mercy!"

Indeed it would be and I said count me in.

We knew that the trip to visit Otto would provide a touchstone for our own alcoholic consumption and mental condition. Otto's presence would be a warning sign on our own slippery slope.

The nurse told us we could find Otto in the cafeteria. We walked in and spotted Otto in the corner with another guy. He seemed surprised and then delighted by our visit. Otto shook our hands and took us to a room to wait while he had his lunch. Malachy said to me, "He doesn't want us to see him eat."

It seemed perfectly normal to me, in fact Otto looked positively full of vim and vigor other than a couple missing teeth in front, which he hid with a sloped grin. Malachy and I had long since lost our hair but Otto was still sporting a mane like Bat Matterston.

The room Otto had escorted us to contained a couch and two chairs, a couple prints on the wall, and a bookcase of old books and arcane magazines like Reader's Digest. It was only about six feet wide and provided just the right amount of claustrophobia for a visit to the mental home.

One of the prints on the wall was a Van Gogh. He was nuts too.

Mack and I catalogued our reaction to Otto's state of mind as we waited.

"He remembered our names!"

"He looks pretty good."

"He's faking."

But Mack was more inclined to give Otto the benefit of the doubt. He had known Otto a lot longer than I and he was still convinced that his boyhood friend was bonkers.

But I had my doubts. This was a compassionate visit but also a research project. If Otto was pretending to be mentally deficient in order to suckle at the county teat and have all his responsibilities disappear, then I was ready to build him a statue.

By the end of our visit that day, Otto's state of mind was still a mystery. Maybe it always will be. And maybe that's how Otto will make sure that Malachy and I will continue to visit our old friend every year until we are as loony as he is. Happy New Year Otto.

THE NEVER FAIL NOVENA

Irish American News
February 2006

The handsome young actor trotted through the falling snow on 49th Street in Manhattan and into St. Malachy's Catholic church. In Gotham it was known as the "actors chapel". The dashing gentleman thespian had been married there only a few years before this visit.

Our hero was out of work and had a wife and two kids at home to feed, clothe, and educate. He was up against it financially and he was once again questioning the wisdom of his career choice in show biz. He was tapioca.

He entered the vestibule and shook the snow from his rugged shoulders as he doffed his cap. It was a dark winter afternoon and there were about ten people scattered through the pews praying. The church was warm and welcoming, a refuge. A homeless guy slept in a pew in front of the statue of the Blessed Virgin Mary.

The actor slid onto a kneeler and made himself comfortable. He was about to engage God in a serious conversation about his future, direction, and salvation. He folded his hands in prayer and asked,
"Why can't I make any money in show biz, God?"

The homeless guy snorted in his sleep a few pews away. The actor looked at him thinking, "That guy was probably once a great Shakespearian actor!"

The homeless fella farted and smacked his lips in his sleep, "Ahh forsooth."

Our hero glanced back to the crucifix and thanked the Lord for the gift of laughter. He looked down into the pew in front of him and saw a small piece of paper lying out on the wooden seat. He picked it up and read the prayer.

The Never Fail Novena
May the Sacred Heart of Jesus be praised, adored, and glorified now and forever throughout the whole world. Most Sacred Heart of Jesus I put my trust in you. Holy Mary, mother of Jesus, pray for me. St. Theresa, child of Jesus, pray for me. St. Jude, Helper of Hopeless Cases, pray for me and grant this favor I ask.

Underneath the prayer was the following notation:
Say this prayer nine times a day for nine days and publish. It has NEVER known to fail. J.S.

The young man looked around for whoever left the message. Nobody was paying any attention, the rest of them transfixed in their own reverie. Who was J. S? And what do they mean by "publish"?

Could whomever left this message on the pew consider that "publishing"? Well, actually it was in a way. The message had found it's way to the young man and he was reading it.

Over the next nine days he carried the novena in his pocket and spoke the prayer in silence along with his request. He wasn't asking to win the lottery. He just wanted to find his way.

Pretty soon he had it memorized and could be seen mumbling the Never Fail Novena as he nursed a beer in his favorite Ninth Avenue bar.

He made copies of the prayer and left them in the pews of St. Malachy's. Those nine days soon turned into ninety, then nine years and then nineteen. He had survived and his family thrived. The Never Fail Novena wasn't said every day, it was only pulled out for nine-day marathons when things began to look grim; when the tapioca got really lumpy.

He often wondered, "Who is J.S.?" and conjectured that maybe it was St. Jude."

Maybe his last name was Sullivan?"

St. Jude supposedly became the patron saint of hopeless cases because so many folks were confused by his name, it sounded too much like Judas. So nobody wanted to pray to dread Judas and just to be on the safe side, they didn't bother with Jude either. So he beefed to God, "What's the point of being a saint if nobody asks me for help?"

God said, "You are hopeless. Hey, that's it; you can be the patron saint of all the hopeless cases, the long shots. And I'll throw in patron saint of cops too!"

God and Saint Jude then cooked up the Never Fail Novena for those long shot sinners. God said, "We'll make it pay off in nine days!'

Jude looked at the prayer and said to God, "Who is J.S.? John Smith?"

God said, "Just Somebody."

The Never Fail Novena never fails to test your faith. The blessings you receive are in direct proportion to your belief. Put Jesus, his blessed mother, St. Theresa and St. Jude on your bench and you're gonna have a pretty good fourth quarter, no matter what the game.

The actor and his family continued to thrive. He kept the Never Fail Novena as the mightiest arrow in his quiver as he aged. He eventually published it officially in an Irish newspaper years later. It has never failed him.

Just somebody is spreading the word. Check it out, The Never Fail Novena pays off in nine days.

SOMETHING FISHY

Irish American News
March 2006

Caller ID came to my rescue. It wasn't the first time I'd hesitated before answering the phone to check and see if I knew the caller. Odds are better if I don't recognize the name because I'm more likely to pick up if I'm sure I don't owe you money.

I used to dread the ring of the phone back when bill collectors would hound me night and day. "Mr. Hooligan, this is Mr. Dunn from Citibank." Calling, no doubt, to dun me.

Once they had you on the line you were trapped, or so I thought. You had to pretend that yes I will pay you right away, Mr. Dunn, just as soon as my check gets here from the professional bowlers pension fund.

An old pal of mine called me the other day at my office. I saw his name on the caller ID, "Trout Kelly".

Trout is an eccentric wizard whose magical powers had been almost entirely destroyed by the tendency to consume tureens of loudmouth soup. He would most certainly be an entertaining conversation if you were in the proper mood. And that particular day I was in a pretty good mood so I answered the phone.

Trout did not disappoint. His calls usually consisted of him reciting a list of all the bastards he was going to expose in a plot that involved a labyrinth of political intrigue. He would deliver his litany of astounding theories and schemes in a breakneck patter that he punctuated constantly with "You understand what I'm sayin'?"

"Yeah" was all you had time for before Trout would pick up the pace of the conversation and be yakking ninety miles a minute. Occasionally he would rest to breathe, while mumbling, "Ya know what I mean? blah blah blah."

The other day when I answered Trout's call I had time on my hands and felt like listening to his cockamamie theories. I was surprised to learn that he had no grand scheme in the works and was just calling to shoot the breeze. He didn't sound loaded as he did many other times and he seemed quite rational. We chatted for a good half hour.

A few days later he called back and it was a different story. I could hear the ice clinking in his glass while he ranted and screamed "Blah...blah...blah!" Uh oh, the Trout had once again jumped out of the boat and into the drink. He was making absolutely no sense and I said, "Trout, I gotta go, I'll call ya back."

Ten minutes later he called back, but I didn't answer. Caller ID had helped me stop him from pirating my precious time. He called several times that day and even left a few messages where he cursed me out and told me his true feelings for our long friendship. I felt sorry for the poor guy as I listened to my voice mail later that day. The booze had ol' Trout in a stranglehold.

Over the years I'd told Trout he should seek help but he always insisted his problem wasn't the drink but a chemical imbalance he had to self-medicate with John Barleycorn. And when he did, he got telephonitis and began calling everybody under the sun to tell them what a-holes they were.

The late night calls were the worst. Many Chicagoans would lie in bed at night praying that Trout would lose their number.

And then along came Caller ID and it kind of put the Trout out of business. I was curious about this marvelous invention and was recently able to get a hold of the inventor of Caller ID. His name is Professor Isadore Dare of the Institute of Furrowed Brows.

How did you come up with this wonderful invention Professor?

"Please, call me Izzy."

Izzy Dare?

"No, he isn't. Yuk yuk yuk. But seriously I came up with the concept of Caller ID to foil the late night calls of my wife's brother, who would drink a case of Schmelkin juice and ring us up to sing the Hebrew National anthem."

I see, so once again, necessity is the mother of invention. Caller ID was invented by Izzy Dare to thwart Schmelkin juice induced calling.

"Well yeah, that and the fact that Trout Kelly had my home number!"

Thank you Professor, please pass me the Schmelkin juice.

PICKLE THE PUGILIST

Irish American News
July 2006

Had dinner in Gotham with boxing legend Angelo Dundee last month. Yeah, it was pretty cool.

Mike "Pickle" Joyce set it up. It was the eve of Tommy Zbikowski's professional boxing debut at Madison Square Garden. Tommy is captain of the fighting Irish football squad and he was fighting on the under card of the

Cotto vs. Malagnaggi welterweight championship of the world. Pickle represents Tommy and a few other contenders.

After a gigantic steak and couple of Manhattans at an east side Steakhouse I rode back to their hotel with Pick and Ang.

The colossal black limo cruised down Broadway through Times Square and I looked at the pugilistic mugs of Dundee and Joyce, descending generations of the sweet science. Angelo talked of his boyhood and how he originally got into the boxing game. I said, "So Ang, are you any relation to Crocodile Dundee?"

My wisecrack fell flatter than Tyson kissing the canvas at the hands of Buster Douglas.

We smoked a cigar at the hotel and Angelo hit the hay. Pickle had the limo all night so we hopped back in and met up with a colorful crew of Chicago characters who were in town for the fight.

Earlier that night I had called Pickle's cell phone and the guy on the other end said, "Pickle's busy, this is Killer, who's this?"

Killer turned out to be Southsider John Kilmartin, Pickle's head of security assigned to keep the girls away from his fighter. Pat Santoro, father and son, were in town for the fight. So were Marty and Oliver McGarry, Danny Joyce, and a murder's row of south side characters. Even Tyson's former ring man Kevin Rooney stumbled through our midst.

On the Peninsula Hotel terrace we quenched our thirst, looked out at the Manhattan skyline and traded boxing stories. I went to the bar for a beer and the bartender said,

"That'll be thirteen dollars."

Thirteen bucks for a light beer?

"That's right."

Where's your gun pal, because thirteen bucks for a beer is criminal behavior. I paid up and told the guy, "That's a ten dollar tip in Chicago." and strolled back outside in search of a host. Brad O'Halloran told me he bought a round that cost him a mortgage payment. Only suckers beef.

I took it on the Arthur T. Duffy, weaved to the elevators, and out into the streets. My weekend in Gotham was in full tilt.

The Fitzpatrick Hotel at 56th and Lexington was my headquarters, thanks to the great hospitality of John Fitzpatrick. He sold the inn he owned in Chicago but John has a pair of jewels in Manhattan, where Irish welcomes keep you comfortable in the elegance of Fitz's castles.

My suite was palatial, with a wet bar, canopy bed, and a bathroom the size of Giant's Causeway. Terrific toilet paper too.

I dropped by the Garden Saturday morning and picked up press credentials for my ringside seats, covering the event for the millions of Irish American News readers. Ace photographer and horseplayer Chris Hart came in from New Jersey to represent the IA News as well. There were eleven fights on the card that night, but Tommy Z was our main event.

Tommy was the last fight before the actual main event and the Notre Dame hype had built this contest into something bigger than the return of the Gipper.

Somebody was doing a helluva promotion job and Pickle Joyce's fingerprints were all over this brilliant brouhaha. Pickle coaches the Leo high school boxing team as well as managing a number of fighters with Marty McGarry. Joyce is also an attorney and it was his keen Irish logic that convinced the NCAA that Zbikowski should go pro. ND football coach Charlie Weiss said, "It's a great summer job for the kid."

So Tommy Zbikowski, a kid who quarterbacked Buffalo Grove high school, was stepping out on the world's stage. My pal, veteran newspaperman "Stormy", summed it up perfectly when he said, "A great place America. Here's a certified Polack in a predominately Irish-German lily-white suburb who goes to high school with a bunch of Jewish princesses and winds up as a head-banging football jock at Notre Dame. Now the story gets better. He's bordering on stardom at South Bend and hooks up with a South Side boxing guru and the next thing you know he's scheduled for his first professional fight, not in Palookaville but in the Valhalla of boxing greats...New Yawks Madison Square Garden, da Godden no less."

Yeah Stormy, it's a movie. Cue Barbara Stanwyck.

Tommy Z's opponent at the Garden that night seemed like an afterthought. Big black dude who outweighed the ND captain by a dozen pounds. Tommy knocked the bum out in 49 seconds.

We all headed down the street to Foley's bar for the victory party where it looked like the entire Fighting Irish football squad was holding court while waiting for Tommy and Pickle. It was strange seeing the loser's corner man at the party, and he was loaded to the gills to boot. Corner man took a swing at my pal Bubba Lee, whereupon the football team grabbed the mope and threw him into a cab outta town before Tommy's entourage tore him to pieces.

I'm standing in front of the bar with Pat Hickey watching all this nonsense when Mark Vanecko walks up with Tour de France champion Lance Armstrong, yeah ol' one ball himself. What a night!

But the man of the hour, the night, and the entire weekend was Mike Pickle Joyce. You should have seen him in the ring at the Garden wearing shades as he draped a towel over the victorious shoulders of Tommy Z. He had orchestrated this entire experience with panache and a cast of characters right out of a Damon Runyon story. I've seen some theatrical extravaganzas in my day, but the weekend in Gotham for the Tommy Z. fight was nonpareil. Thanks Pickle.

CAMP SPELLBOUND

Irish American News
August 2006

In the good ol' summertime many folks from the Chicago area like to drive several hours into Northern Wisconsin for some fishing, swimming, and drinking.

People in Wisconsin love this because it gives them someone to hate. I first noticed this as two guys in mullets passed me on the left in a pickup truck as they flipped me the bird on the highway. "What's eatin' those guys", I wondered.

They must have seen my plates. The farther you go up north in Wisconsin the louder the culture clash. But the tranquility of the woods and lakes can be therapeutic and when my old pal John Spellman invited me for some fishing a few weeks ago I said,"That's just what I need, some r' and 'r."

Yes it was restful, like resting among the bears would be for a rube from the city.

Spellman and I had an apartment at the corner of Wellington and Broadway in our college days, "the insanity of 1970-72". We were hippies, mostly for the fringe benefits. Spellman was known in those days as "Spellbound", a name he attributed to his hypnotic power over the minds of the ladies he loved. I'm more inclined to think the Spellbound alias could be traced to the film "Spellbound", an old Hitchcock thriller starring Gregory Peck as a man slowly going insane. The name fit.

Spellbound is just another portly old grizzly like me these days. As we fished on his lake Spellbound would take calls from his new girlfriend. He hangs up the phone and shrugs with a chuckle, "She likes fat old bald guys... And I'm glad she does!"

I arrived late on a Thursday night and Spellbound took me immediately to the Breezy Point bar and grill. They stayed open late for us. Oh yeah, did I tell you Wisconsin is also known for beer. And shots.

Breezy Point became our headquarters during my Wisconsin sojourn. One night we were rocking out at the bar and I went to play some tunes on the juke box. I ask the bar what number I should play and an old lady three stools down, says to me, "I like 69."

That's naughty grandma. You don't look a day over 68.

The Spellman family has a rustic home and spread right on the lake with a bunkhouse across the road that sleeps a dozen more. Spellbound is an avid sportsman; a hunter of wild animals, and not just the Oregon State mascot either. He fishes too and won a Walleye tournament in Madison the week before my visit to "Camp Spellbound."

Spellbound and I returned to camp that night and met his brother Frank and stepbrother Dennis Butkus. Spellbound told them of the huge bear he saw on the road the day before, "just starin' at me." Lindsay Lohan appeared on the TV and the room fell silent.

Finally Spellbound stands up and says, "I wanna show you guys something."

Spellbound's opening remark in the bars we hit was always, "Seen any bears lately?" That got everybody talking. It's a bear's world and we're just livin' in it. I'd been hearing bear stories all night and I half expected Spellbound to pop out of the kitchen now in a bear suit.

Instead he brought a deer back from the freezer.

"Check this out, twenty pounds of venison."

Butkus the chef grabs it for examination and proclaims in jubilation, "This is back strap! Back strap man!" If he could have done a back flip without hurting himself, he would have. Evidently back strap is the tenderest part of Bambi.

She was delicious, like steak but with a little snap to it.

Spellbound and I actually caught fish in between beers and boating. On Saturday the brothers took me skeet shooting in a sand pit a few miles away. Frank hands me the shotgun and says, "Try a few Mike."

I put the gun to my shoulder and fired both barrels. Suddenly all the beer and Baileys I'd had the night before began to percolate. Uh oh, I better not do that again. If a shotgun doesn't shake something loose, nothin' will. It was a blast, but almost a blast in my khaki shorts.

I retreated to the hammock along the lake at Camp Spellbound, a lovely spot where I could nap, read, or pretend to sleep when any of those guys looked like they might ask me to help them lift something. It was idyllic; birds crapped on me while I slept.

Camp Spellbound was rejuvenating, particularly the conversation. The director of maintenance of the camp is a Walter Brennan type guy in overalls with a Billy goat beard named Rudy. He told me of a bear that had been terrorizing campers and was finally caught and killed. They hung the bear by its feet from a tree for all to see. The guy told Rudy the bear was 27 years old. Rudy asked him how he could tell. "We counted the rings in his a..hole."

On the day I left I noticed the netting of the hammock was now all stretched out with a huge divot where a fat bear may have snoozed. Yeah it was fun, just being a bear.

Spellbound & Rudy

DICK DOODY'S WAKE

Irish American News
October 2006

"Fred C. Dobbs" was just one of the many aliases used by the man who lay
in his coffin in the party room of Jenny's Steakhouse.

Dick Doody, an old pal from around the mahogany of Ken's bar on Western avenue, had croaked and left a last will and testament that provided for
a final party. He picked the location, paid for the drinks, and his corpse was
saluted with toasts all night long. It was The Southside event of the summer.

I'd known him for years as a jovial chum, but his wake revealed tales of a
shady past. Dick was 72. The Southtown said he died of "unknown causes".

His cousin Larry told me stories of them as kids on the south side, but that didn't explain how he went on to become one of Chicago's most infamous sportsmen.

I spent a day with Fred C. Dobbs at the track and watched him win five grand on a trifecta while juggling his cell phone and taking action on the football games. The guy just really loved sports.

I asked an ex-cop at the wake about Dobbsy's past and he told me, "He lived in Vegas for years, moved back here about 15 years ago. I think he's still wanted for something in Nevada."

Rollie Keane said Dobbsy apologized to him late one night in Ken's. "He said he was sorry for sticking up a Keane gas station early in his career."

Dick was a fan of the John Huston classic film, "Treasure of the Sierra Madre", a story of greed and murder among gold prospectors. Humphrey Bogart played Fred C. Dobbs, a man who loses his mind and morality in the hot sun. Dick Doody would quote Fred C. Dobbs throughout the night as he sat at the bar.

When Dobbsy's glass was empty he would just sit on his stool and shout in a booming voice, "Thirsty!"

The other doppelganger for Dick Doody was the character played by Jimmy Cagney in "White Heat". Early in the morning, after a long night at the bar, Doody would become "Cody Jarrett", screaming from the top of a water tower with guns blazing, "Top of the world ma!"

Dobbs bought the farm in bed, and in the nightstand drawer was a note with instructions for his wake. Put me in the party room at Jenny's Steakhouse. Call Carl Courtwright the owner; he'll set it up.

Carl told me, "Yeah, he originally wanted to be sitting up in his coffin with a drink in his hand." The village of Chicago Ridge got wind of that and said ixnay. The Mayor insisted that Dobbsy's casket be closed and in a room away from the food.

The Mayor didn't want dead Dobbsy anywhere near the food. Plenty of folks were mingling around the casket with drinks in their hands though. It was a great atmosphere to reminisce about our old friend.

I grabbed a ham sandwich in the back of the room and washed it down with beer and it never tasted better than that night in Dobbsy's presence.

Andy McGann handled the prep for Dobbs' wake and Jenny's was jammed with friends and admirers of Fred C. Dobbs. Ellie Riley Delaplane toasted her old friend.

How did you meet Fred C. Dobbs, Ellie?

"He went on my honeymoon with me."

Dobbsy was laid out by the fireplace and on the mantel was a copy of a poem an old pal had written. Fred C. Dobbs was his hero, and he stayed out of the way of Cody Jarret.

I grabbed a beer at the bar and Bill Gainer said to us, "Fred C. Dobbs was an honest man."

On the next stool, policeman George Gobel agreed, "He was brutally honest!" A fitting epitaph.

It was a happy group of Southsiders at Dobbsy's wake. Jack Casto, Jimmy Sexton, Skip Carey, and Jack Wright shed no tears for their old buddy Dobbs. He wouldn't have wanted it any other way.

Billy Gainer announced, "This could start a whole new trend, 'wake and steak'. I might do this for my wake. I'm lookin' forward to it!"

Gobel deadpanned, "Yeah, we can't wait."

James T. Goff walked into the wake and ordered a drink. The legends are dying off but we've still got Goff. He's got the DNA of a New York City cockroach. You walk into the lounge in Hell and Jimmy Goff will be sittin' at the bar.

"Goff balls" and Frankie Mo toasted Dobbs and we all clinked our beers. Thank you Dobbsy, for the great time and for the drinks. Mo raised his glass and pronounced, "To Fred C. Dobbs, he was a sport 'til the very end!"

AN IGNOBLE DEATH

Irish American News
November 2006

How do you want to die?

Come on, you've thought about it. Or at least heard details of somebody's death and said to yourself, "What a way to go!"

I was watching an old Abbot & Costello movie the other night and Boris Karlov was this creepy guy who hypnotizes Lou Costello and tries to get him to commit suicide. After several unsuccessful comic attempts at getting Lou to either hang himself or jump out the hotel room window, Boris asks in exasperation, "Okay how would you do it? How do you want to die?"

Lou stands on the windowsill of the 20th floor of the Waldorf in his pajamas with a noose around his neck and hypnotically says, "Old age."

Plenty of wise guys will tell you they want to go out like the late actor John Garfield, who supposedly died in the saddle. The late Vice-President Nelson Rockefeller passed that way too.

Old Rocky threw a seven while doing the nasty with his "staff assistant", Megan Marshak. He was 70, she was 25. It was a heart attack waiting to happen. Rocky's wife, Happy, wasn't too happy about the news and had Rocky cremated less than 24 hours later.

Ever the gent, Rocky left Megan fifty grand in his will. Thanks for the "grabber".

Many of us want death to come in an instant, unexpectedly, without any pain.

Somebody sneaks up on you from behind and blows your head off with a shotgun. It's over before you even know what hit ya. My pal Pete Nolan told me he wants to go in his sleep, after a round of golf and some drinks as he naps on his couch. Nice and comfy.

Elderly folks of faith look forward to their demise. There's a great scene in "Grumpy Old Men" when Jack Lemmon says to Walter Mathau, "Hear about Fred? He dropped dead of a heart attack last night."

Mathau continues shoveling his walk and says, "That lucky bastard!"

Which brings me to the case of the poor mope who fell out of a tree in Englewood last month. The Sun-Times said, "Julian Spencer was adept at climbing trees as a young boy in his native Jamaica."

Julian died in a comic tragedy. He was horsing around at a pal's house at 64th and Racine. Maybe he was shooting his mouth off about what a great tree climber he was when one of his buddies bet him twenty bucks he couldn't scale the tree in the yard in front of them.

Julian took off his shoes and handed his wallet to 62-year-old friend Lawrence Williams. The Sun-Times carried a photo of Lawrence in front of the offending tree. He looked like Redd Foxx.

Up the tree went Julian, six feet, eight feet, ten feet, twelve feet, he climbed. He got about 15 feet up and a branch cracked under him and he tumbled down and hit his head on the concrete. Good night.

Somebody asked his friend Lawrence Williams why he didn't catch him, but it happened too fast. Julian died of head injuries at the hospital later that night. I hope he didn't suffer.

Killjoys would say, "What the hell was a 49 year old man doing climbing a tree at night, was he drunk?"

Nope, just drinking water on an Indian summer night.

"Well, he had no business climbing a tree, serves him right. The death of a fool!"

I wonder.

I think Julian probably climbed the tree to entertain his friends. Julian was alive that night, living and breathing and jiving his pals. He went out on a limb for his buddies.

I'll bet St. Peter ushered Julian directly to the VIP room in heaven, where scientists, performers, poets, athletes, and artists mingle in greatness. Julian met legendary historical figures who had climbed their own metaphorical trees on earth. They saw challenges before them and up the tree they went.

Julian's pal Lawrence Williams told the Sun-Times, "I never saw anything like it in my life."

Up in heaven Julian Spencer is partying with Jonas Saulk, Edison, Jackie Robinson, Dr. Martin Luther King, JFK, St. Joan, Galileo, and Jayne Mansfield. Tree Climbers all!

Julian Spencer, I salute you! You died a noble death...as opposed to Rocky.

CHAPTER ELEVEN
2007

PADDY'S DAY '07

Irish American News
April 2007

Thank God it will be another seven years at least before St. Patrick's Day falls on a Saturday night again. Uh…wait….I guess with leap year it will only be….uh….ah…never mind, my brain is still fried from the madness of last March.

The annual St. Patrick's Day jig begins as early as late January when the Parade Committee has their corned beef and cabbage dinner at Plumber's Hall. That's like spring training for Chicago's Hibernians.

A couple weeks later is the prologue of the season when the parade Queen is elected on a Sunday afternoon in mid February. Chicago's Irish beauties are examined by a group of plumbers, politicians, and McGaffers.

When the queen is crowned around 5:30PM on a Sunday, that's the starting shot of the Paddy's day marathon, which lasted about three weeks this year. It wasn't easy, but we did it!

Knowing of the endurance I would need, I forsook the beer for the south side parade. Never again! My thirst was intense but the long ride home had me spooked. Next time I'm getting a designated driver.

And that's what I did for St. Patrick's Day, just six days later. My old pal in Galway, Mike Monaghan, is friends with The Saw Doctors and Mike got me tickets for their concert at the Vic that night.

I enlisted the aid of Mr. Richie Golz, an old pal since we were caddies at Beverly CC in the early sixties. Richie is the perfect wheelman. He's always prepared with bottled water and bucket seats. He's a member of Mensa, who once loaned me his membership card for a story I wanted to do on their Halloween party, "Mensa Undercover." My glasses were my costume.

In honor of the Paddy's Day rock concert I had donned my green cowboy boots from the play, "Mickey Finn". That was seven years and forty pounds ago. Even my feet are fatter now, so I asked Richie to stop by my office downtown while I went upstairs and clipped my toenails in preparation for a night of stumbling.

As we drove to The Vic for the show, the streets were filled with green garlanded youths, most of them inebriated. I saw a young man caressing the neck of his best gal while she bent down and barfed on the sidewalk. I rolled down the window and chirped, "Happy St. Patrick's Day!" He cursed me as we peeled away.

IA News publisher Cliff Carlson joined us for a pre-concert drink. We walked into a joint next to 1000 Liquors on Belmont. It was wall to wall with Generation X'ers who had been boozin' all day. We had a whiskey and left for the theatre. That was the last I saw of Cliff that night.

I had an extra four tickets that I sold to a couple of black Irishmen in front of the Vic. Eddie Murphy's twins would sell them later for more, but it was quick beer money for me, so I was feelin' groovy as the security guards frisked us on the way in.

That's when we found out the seating was general admission, and the entire first floor of the Vic was one huge mosh pit of crocked Celts. Richie and I grabbed a beer and opted for the balcony seats. The crowd was a generational mix of Micks. Cliff must have been swallowed up in the soup of potato heads. I saw one guy on the edge of the mosh pit who looked to be in his seventies.

I said to Richie, "That guy's going to get lucky tonight!"

"I doubt it," chortled the Mensa man.

The Saw Doctors put on a terrific show, and the audience was filled with fans that seemed to know the lyrics of every tune. Our seats were great and only a few feet from the beer stand and men's room. Mindy the bartender told a lady who was beefing about paying four bucks for a bottle of water, "Just fill it up in the bathroom sink when you're done, our tap water is excellent."

She says this just as I return from the loo and a chaotic scene of sink pid-
dling. Thanks for the tip, Mindy. I'll stick to the beer.

When Elvis performed in concert women would throw their panties
onstage. At the Saw Doctors show, somebody in the crowd tossed an Irish
tri-color pair of boxers with a fake butt sewn on the back. The musicians
held them up to show the crowd and the place went nuts.

After the show, Richie and I waded through the beer cups in the empty
mosh pit and found the drawers in question. There was a pair of red lips
painted on the left cheek and the Gaelic words that capture my heart every
St. Patrick's Day, "Pog Mo Thon!"

Hope you had as much fun as we did. Thanks Saw Doctors, for a great
Chicago St. Patrick's Day 2007.

Aftermath of the Sawdoctors concert

KITTY CARLISLE HART

Irish American News
May 2007

I watched her on TV when I was a kid, "What's My Line" and "To Tell the Truth". She was the lady in the evening gown whose name, "Kitty", belied her high society sophistication.

I never dreamed then that I would some day mortify her guests with my raunchy behavior at a party in her home. Kitty Carlisle was Broadway royalty and as close to the monarchy that I would ever get.

I was tapioca when my sons were born in New York in 1980 and I cooked up a scheme to teach producing to make some quick cash. I put an ad in Variety for my "Off-Broadway Producer's Seminar" and ten suckers…I mean students… signed up for the class.

Each student filled out a questionnaire detailing their background in show business and answered a series of my questions to determine if they had any dough. I glanced through them and was pleased to discover that one of my students was the son of the late, legendary playwright and director Moss Hart. Jackpot!

Chris Hart was the same age as me and we became partners in producing and pals for the rest of our lives. I tried to get my hands on his silver spoon and wound up with stardust. I learned far more from him over the years than any tricks I taught. Trusting his taste, I asked him to direct "Goin' East on Ashland". He made it a hit.

Chris and I spoke on the phone just last week when the news hit that his mother, the indomitable Kitty Carlisle Hart, died at the age of 96.

She had an astonishing career in opera, theatre, TV, and films, and even appeared as the ingénue in the Marx Brothers comedy "A Night at the Opera". Broadway dimmed their lights in her honor the night after she died.

Back in the early eighties Chris Hart, Frank Cento and I had an office on Broadway, producing comedies and living one as well. I first met his mother, Kitty Carlisle Hart, when she dropped by to check out our space.

I was a little intimidated by this doyenne of the American theatre visiting our dumpy headquarters. She was chairwoman of the NY State Council of the Arts then and her power was palatable. Frank Cento dubbed her "The Kittster" that day, and it became our pet name for her, whenever she wasn't around.

The Kittser!

Kitty wasn't too impressed with our digs but deemed them decent as she gazed out the window looking down on "the street of dreams". She pointed out theatres below where she had starred in some of the all time classics of Broadway. She called each of us "darling" and wanted to know our plans.

We had optioned a play about a reunion of Gerry Ford, Nixon, and Gordon Liddy playing poker in Ford's basement entitled "The Basement Tapes". The Kittster rattled off a list of potential investors for us and left Chris with a kiss on the cheek. We were in business, show business!

Basement Tapes opened at the Village Gate in September of '83. Since most of our investors were her friends, Kitty Carlisle hosted our opening night party at her lavish home on Madison Avenue in Gotham.

My brother Bobo was in town for the show and he came to the Kittster's house with me that night. We drank with Swifty Lazar and he told us the show had "legs" while Arlene Francis, Martin Gable and dozens of other show biz personalities schmoozed with the cast. That was Kitty's crowd.

At her daughter Kathy's wedding I met Claudette Colbert, Betty Comden & Adolph Green, and a guy who introduced himself as "Hi I'm Hugh Carey and this is my wife Angie."

It was none other than the Governor of New York who had just married the Greek condo tycooness from Chicago before discovering that he was her fourth husband. She looked at me like I was something on the bottom of her shoe and pulled Hugh away into the crowd.

On opening night it's customary to wait for the reviews to come in and the first one was on television. The TV critic, a mope by the name of Stuart Klein, thought he would be funny by doing a Nixon impersonation to open his review of The Basement Tapes. All the luminaries huddled into Kitty's den to watch the review. Klein came on the tube with his Tricky Dick, "Let me make one thing perfectly clear…this show stinks!"

The rest of his review was even worse and the air was sucked right out of that room as we watched in stunned horror. That's when my old south side instincts kicked in and I screamed at the TV, "F—— you! You f—-in' #%*^#!"

Jaws dropped collectively.

My lovely wife Mary grabbed me at that point and said, "We better get out of here." As we walked to the elevator, one of Kitty's gentlemen friends said to me, "I don't think those words have ever been uttered in this house."

While I may have shocked her guests that night I never heard a complaint from the Kittster. Chris and I kept on producing flops but the Kittster was always encouraging.

I was up for a job in Chicago with the Illinois Arts Council and she sent them a telegram extolling my talents. She said, "What do you want me to tell them, Houli darling?"

Kitty Carlisle was performing her one-woman show up until just weeks before her death. Show Business will never see her like again, a 96-year-old grand dame singing and dancing her heart out onstage. She touched more than a million hearts and I was lucky enough to be one of them.

THE DEATH OF THE CAA

Irish American News
June 2007

Groucho Marx famously said, "I would not join any club that would have someone like me for a member."

Seventeen years ago I joined the Chicago Athletic Association and now it's tanking. Like a mighty ship run aground on an iceberg, it's taking on water and rats are scrambling all over the deck.

The CAA was founded in 1890 as a "gentlemen's club", and while that description nowadays is a euphemism for bawdyhouse; the CAA dripped with class for over a hundred years. Members included some of Chicago's most prominent Irishmen who availed themselves of the first class athletic, dining, and drinking amenities provided by the club.

I first entered its marbled stairway when I was ten years old. Jim Havey's dad was a member and he sponsored Jim's pals for the Saturday morning kids program.

We'd get up early on Saturdays and hop the Rock Island to LaSalle Street station. We'd walk over to Michigan Avenue and spend the day boxing, shooting baskets, and swimming at the CAA.

On the way home we'd all chip in and get one of the sailors in the train station to buy us a Playboy magazine. Those were the halcyon days of our youth.

Those memories of the CAA established an early appreciation for the finer things in life; the history and tradition of sport, the camaraderie of a locker room, cigars and beer.

In its infancy the CAA had sent teams to battle on the gridiron with Harvard, Yale, and other Universities. In the early 1900's the CAA sponsored many athletes in the Olympics, and several members to this day are Olympians. The dining halls and locker rooms were adorned with trophies from past triumphs and this kid thought it was just about the coolest thing he'd ever seen.

When I was 40 I dropped by the CAA to reminisce one day while walking down Michigan Avenue. It was just as I remembered it and I decided then and there to apply for membership. To my surprise they let me in, maybe because I had clout-heavy sponsors in Tom Gibbs and Phil Rock. The dues weren't exorbitant and since I was in the business of raising money for my theatrical ventures I figured it might help to hang out with rich people even though I wasn't rich myself.

I started working out but mostly just having fun with my kids in the gym or having dinner in the elegant dining room that looked out on the lake. I liked hanging at the Cherry Circle bar too, where I could put on a nice package before heading for the train.

And my instincts were right about finding money. I met lots of investors at the CAA who rolled the dice with me onstage and I made tons of friends.

But things started to unravel after about ten years. I was able to finagle an office in the CAA building itself and now I could work, nap, swim, and drink all on the same day in the same building.

I was sitting pretty until I tried to hook up my phone service. Turns out two members of the CAA board of directors, let's call them Klinger and Vlasic, had some sort of monopoly on the phone service.

They sent their fat secretary to my door one day and she handed me a bill and screeched at me for the shoddy workmanship of my phone installer. Of course I told her what she could do with her invoice and also sent her bosses a letter telling them I had no intention of paying, with what I thought were some amusing comments about their gal Friday's girth.

They were not amused and one of these twits pounded on my door with a butter knife in his hand and threatened to cut off my phone service. Things were getting ugly at the CAA and they just got worse from that day on.

I never paid them and Klinger and Vlasic put a motion before the board to oust me from the club citing me as a "sexist". Wow, that was a real news flash.

The board, in its wisdom, voted no. It might have been the only sensible thing that board of directors ever did. Years went by and the CAA suddenly announced to its membership that the club was almost broke and needed an emergency infusion of cash.

If you paid a couple grand you became an A member and retained your vote; or you could not pay and remain a non-voting B member. I decried this class warfare at the annual meeting and proclaimed, "You are creating an aristocracy!"

"Tut-tut" were the words of the majority and they went ahead and created the new class system. I paid up only to protect my vote because I still remembered those blagguards trying to blackball me. Then things got worse.

An investigation of the board revealed that Klinger and Vlasic had been stealing from the membership through an intricate set of nefarious rent and telephone deals and the club was on the brink of bankruptcy. They were expelled from the CAA, oh sweet justice!

But they had left a gaping wound that could not be healed.

The building was put up for sale and now the venerable old CAA is in its final days. Lawsuits are flying in all directions with B members suing for a piece of the pie and it looks like attorneys will wind up eating all but the crumbs.

It's all going to go, the furniture, the trophies, the spittoons, the history of a grand old club where Chicago's Irish spilled booze over their lace curtains.

What killed it? The end of expense accounts? Smokers and drinkers becoming pariah? I know those bastards Klinger and Vlasic had a lot to do with it, but in the end I guess all the members should blame themselves for not keeping a closer eye on the people running the joint.

I think we were all just having too much fun to pay that much attention. I guess Groucho was right after all.

GOTHAM WEEKEND

Irish American News
July 2007

Toora Loora Looral has nothin' on the lullaby of Broadway. Like a siren's song it draws me back to Gotham every so often. I took the lovely Mary back to the ol' wooing grounds just last week and it was an adventure.

We were headed to the Broadway Memorial for Kitty Carlisle Hart who died last month at the age of 96. The strange details of how we got to know "The Kittster" were spelled out in my May column, so dig it out of that pile of old Irish Americans you keep by the throne and try to keep up.

We flew out of Midway and our first stop after the federal frisk was Reilly's Daughter in search of old pal Boz O'Brien. No sign of Boz or his son Brendan but their cousin Jimmy O'Brien entertained us behind the bar while I nursed a screwdriver.

I saw Robin Givens new autobiography on sale at the newsstand and asked Mary, "You think I'm in it?"

I imagined scanning the index for my name and a reference as the honky hunk who strangled her in the ill-fated TV series "Angel Street". Robin's quote, "I got smacked around by Mikes both black and white!"

My darling Mary gave me the window seat on the plane and she wound up squeezed in the middle next to a middle aged bald Baby Huey in the aisle seat with sweat running off his nose for the duration of our flight. I offered to switch seats but she said, "I wouldn't do that to you." What a wonderful wife!

Abdul picked us up at LaGuardia in his Lincoln Town car and we zoomed to Manhattan. Our headquarters would be the Fitzpatrick Hotel at 56th and Lexington. John Fitz is the greatest of hosts and our digs were spectacular.

New York can seem like a third world country as you walk the street and encounter the polyglot of languages and accents of refugees from all over the globe. But when you settle onto a stool at Fitzer's, the cozy pub attached to the Fitzpatrick Hotel, you're among your own again in a friendly Irish saloon.

Our first night in Gotham we were treated to dinner and drinks by our old friends Tom and Ruth Nardini. Tom and I shared a dressing room on Broadway many moons ago. He started out in show biz at 18 as the Indian kid in "Cat Ballou" starring Lee Marvin and Jane Fonda. Studios kept trying to cast him as an Injun from then on but he was really just a California goombah who grew up in Englewood. Tom told me when "Cat Ballou" tested audiences before they opened all over the country, the kids in his old neighborhood stuffed the votes for him and he wound up with an eight year studio contract thanks to his pals.

The memorial for Kitty Carlisle was the next day at the Majestic Theatre on 44th Street. Mary and I walked down the street and discovered a line almost around the block to get in. Kitty's son Chris had invited us so we flashed our invites and waltzed right in and found ourselves among a crowd that I thought didn't exist anymore.

It was old time Broadway all over again and the memorial featured clips from Kitty's movies; scenes with Bing Crosby and the Marx brothers. Mario Cuomo eulogized. So did Mayor Bloomberg, Barbara Walters, and a host of entertainers who sang Kitty's praises. I felt like we were in a time warp when the great white way was at its' peak. We ran into old show biz pals we hadn't seen in over twenty years, including character actor Dave Wohl. Many of you would recognize him from the TV show "Law and Order", where he has a recurring role as a pervert.

We went across the street to Sardi's after the show. Mary and I had our wedding reception there so we reminisced with a couple pals from the bad ol' days. We had made the cut for invitation back to Kitty's home on 62nd Street and Madison, the scene of my crime over 25 years ago. Hobnobbing in The Kittster's living room with the luminaries wasn't much different than anyplace else on the planet that day. Everybody talked of how Paris Hilton deserved more jail time.

That was my cue to launch into one of my favorite old songs taught to me by Joe Howard, "Oh the women's prison...how I wish I was with 'em!"

We rushed back to Fitzer's that night to meet our old pal Jack Whalen, AKA Way-Way. Jack was best man at our wedding and is always entertaining. Way-Way slammed Heinekens while regaling the bar with stories of our youth. He had white hair in sixth grade, which the girls found dashing and liquor store owners found convincing, but these days he looks like the late Senator Everett Dirksen on a bender.

Way-Way in Gotham

Our final day in Gotham was a whirlwind of stops along Fifth Ave, and lunch at the New York Athletic club, which we topped off with a rickshaw ride across town. The driver rode a bike while I plunked my big butt in back and felt sorry for him peddling the load. Most of the drivers are from Africa with names like Oogie. This would be a great racket on the south side of Chicago. I can just see Dogs Daugherty hopping in a rickshaw and announcing, "Take me to the Beverly Woods and step on it, Kunta Kinte!"

We hit St. Patrick's cathedral for mass and on the way out we bumped into Tom Brokaw walking down the street. I shouted out, "Tom, how's it goin'?" He cringed visibly and gave me a wincing acknowledgement.

The guy wants me to welcome him into my living room every night for thirty years and then blanches when I say hello on the street. Well excoooose me, Mr. Bigshot!

Back to the hotel to meet Abdul for our ride to LaGuardia and Mary and I bid adieu to the wonderful hospitality of the Fitzpatrick family. We had a ball but the best part for me was taking my own 'lil Broadway baby, "the lovely Mary Carney" back home.

O LUCKY MAN

Irish American News
October 2007

Bernie Boland's wife Sheila always told him to look on the bright side of things. It was a philosophy Bernie embraced until just last month. That's when his "glass half full" was flung against the wall and shattered into hundreds of mean little shards. Bernie Boland had a bad summer.

In May Bernie was feeling like a champ. He had just weathered another bitter winter and his future was looking up.

He had his annual physical and Doctor Scully gave him a clean bill of health, even giving Bernie an extra prostate exam just to make sure. "Well if you insist Bernie, I'll check it again, bend over."

While he was getting dressed Bernie asked the doc one final question. "I've noticed my nose whistling a lot when I breathe, does that mean anything?"

Dr. Scully got out his physician flashlight and took a peek up Bernie's nostrils. "Holy Toledo, what the hell is that?"

Turns out the Doc found the whistling growth, deemed it cancerous and said Bernie's nose must be removed immediately. On the way back from the hospital Sheila consoled him, "You never liked your nose anyway. Oh look, there's a quarter on the ground!"

In June Bernie was back in business with a prosthetic schnozz and a new attitude. He went to New York with his boss, who was being honored by the Irish American McGaffers Assn. Bernie had written his speech and worked with a biographer on an article on his boss. The night was a big success.

Bernie didn't mind when his boss told him there was no room on the private plane that night. His boss booked him into the plush St. Regis and Bernie looked forward to watching movies all night in his room. But Bernie lost his wallet in the cab and his bank account was empty the next morning. Whoever found it must have figured out Bernie's ATM password, LUCK-YME.

Sheila told Bernie, "Look on the bright side, the plane might have crashed, and you got to watch the new Harry Potter movie for free!"

Bernie's boss fired him in July when he got the bill from the St. Regis, room service up the wazoo and the movies weren't quite in the Harry Potter oeuvre.

Sheila told him, 'This will give you an opportunity to finish that novel you've been working on!"

Bernie finished his book, Poodle Dump Lane, a mystery about the dog-walkers of Lake Point Tower, in August. He bought a Lotto ticket every day and fished off the Monroe Street harbor with his old Chinese friend, Wan Hung Lo. He was just waiting for his ship to come in.

One day Bernie snagged an odd looking fish with six eyes and five fins, a result of BP Amoco dumping ammonia in Lake Michigan. As Bernie struggled to get the freak fish off his hook, a skinhead pushed Wan Hung into the water and he drowned.

Bernie was distraught over his pal's demise but Sheila said, "That fish is going to look great stuffed over our fireplace!"

In September all ten publishers sent rejection letters to Bernie for Poodle Dump Lane. They said it was derivative.

Bernie was indicted as a co-conspirator in the murder of Wan Hung Lo, turned out the skinhead had a good lawyer.

Bernie's old boss filed a lawsuit against him for defamation of character. He didn't like the way he was portrayed in the novel. Bernie had sent him the first copy right after he self-published Poodle Dump Lane.

Instead of mounting the fish back in August, Bernie had cooked and eaten it. Boils broke out all over his face and he began growing a third eye just above his fake nose.

Sheila told Bernie, "Look on the bright side… hey, what the hell are you doing with that axe?"

The winning lotto ticket fell from Bernie's pocket as he hacked her body to pieces on a beautiful fall evening.

BLACKBALLED

Irish American News
November 2007

It's official. At least one institution in this city, (that I know of), has labeled me as "riffraff".

The Union League Club of Chicago has denied my application for membership. The pasty-faced patrician who delivered this news bulletin to me said, "I can't tell you our reasons, that's confidential."

Mister Klenchjaw then said, "You can apply again in six months."

Yeah, thanks Klenchie old boy. Maybe that penis growing out of my forehead will have vanished by then.

I can't say I'm surprised. Ever since the Chicago Athletic Association closed and encouraged all members to go to the Union League, I've been apprehensive. It's a different atmosphere over there. The only thing liberally given out is the eyeball of scrutiny.

The interesting thing is that out of the hundred odd CAA guys who transferred membership to the Union League, only two that I know of were rejected; me and a guy who did time in a Mexican prison for gold smuggling about thirty years ago. And he's a pretty good guy!

I'm not naïve enough to think I haven't made enemies over the years. I'm an outspoken chronicler of hypocrisy and absurdity and I take pride in that. But which of my attributes can take the blame for my blackballing?

I discussed this with my lovely wife a few nights ago and she reeled off a litany of my character traits that could have led to my ostracism.

"Well, maybe it was because you always paid your bill late at the CAA. They could have said you're a deadbeat...or a lush...or maybe it was that draft-dodger thing...or your fatness...you're very crude...your clothes don't fit...or the way you eat like a slob...or..."

That's quite enough, I said, I get the picture. None of that stuff really bothers me. What irritates me the most is that the identity of my accusers is kept secret. I like to know who is out there spreading venom about my character, like to make sure it's true. But the Union League Club has chosen the coward's way of character assassination.

Of course I'm happy now that I couldn't join their club. Who wants to go where they're not wanted? But these schmucks wouldn't even put it in writing, no letter, just the word passed on to me, "Sorry you're not our kind darling."

It's all for the best. I couldn't afford it now anyway. However I would suggest they remove the word "Chicago" from their moniker at the Union League Club. As Eddie Vrdolyak once said, "In Chicago, we don't stab you in the back, we stab you in the front!" Well not these guys.

So I will take pride in their snub and remember my mother's words "the bitter lesson is best taught". It's what I got for sticking my nose into a wasps nest.

Of course I forgive them and even though I may announce to the world that the Union League Club can kiss my fat Irish ass, I'm actually, in my own way, just turning the other cheek.

WILLIE'S CHRISTMAS CHEER

Irish American News
December 2007

I still get drunk on my birthday each December, if I can fit it into my schedule. But the annual enthusiasm of this kid is replaced with the awe of another year going out with a bang to celebrate, not my birthday, but the birthday of Our Lord Savior Jesus Christ.

We always reach out to Lazarus lying in the street around Christmas, seems the right thing to do.

"You gave that crack whore a dollar?"

"Hey man, it's Christmas!"

Guilt doesn't inspire Christmas spirit. It's genuine. The stars twinkling on a cold December night, your breath a puff of smoke, and suddenly you see a stranger on the street, anybody, and you want to help them, a jolt of love emanates from you and you stop and think, "Yeah man, it's Christmas. Cool!"

My dad and my brother Willie came to visit us in New York one Christmas when Mary and I were newlyweds, 1978. It was great having them in town that week picking up our tabs. Willie and Dad stayed at the Barclay and I would come over in the morning and jump on their room service bacon.

On Christmas Eve we drove out to Aqueduct. My old man gave me a C-note before the first race. He was in his seventies then and sent me to the window with his bets. I had no intention of blowing a hundred bucks so I pretended to parlay.

I mistakenly followed Willie to the $50 window, Mr. Big Shot. Standing in front of us was a guy weighing about 400 pounds, sweating, and making lots of bets. Willie eyed the "minutes to post time" as Fatso jawboned with the clerk about a trifecta. My brother turned to me and said, "This fat f—— is gonna get us shut out!"

Uh oh. I had seen my brother Willie's temper before and it was not a pretty sight. He didn't start by being mildly irritated and work his way up; no he would just immediately blow a gasket that would make a whirling dervish duck. It was always accompanied by a stream of profanity that left a toxic cloud of blue vapor hanging in the air.

The track announcer warned over the loudspeakers, "One minute, one minute to post-time."

I immediately fell back and pretended not to know Willie; the disassociation principle. I knew what was coming. I slid into another line just as he let loose on this guy. It was impressive, he called the guy every dirty name I had ever heard in my life and each time it was preceded with "You fat—-" Fill in the blanks, lots of F and C words. Folks tripped over themselves to get away from Willie, me included.

The fat guy waddled away without looking back at my brother. He could have flattened both of us but wanted no part of the dog connected to that bark. Willie stepped up to the window and got his bet down. Taking his ticket, he sneered to the clerk, "Merry Christmas."

That night we went over to my place and celebrated our winnings. Dad and Willie hadn't won but I was up a hundred.

We put my pop in a cab and Mary and I talked Willie into Midnight Mass at St. Malachy's on 49th Street.

St. Malachy's is also known as The Actors Chapel, so they put on a great show with opera performers doing "Oh Holy Night" accompanied by brass sections in the choir loft; trumpets and cymbals along with the carols.

The church was packed and we were lucky to get seats in the last row. A bum was jammed into the aisle seat right in front of us. He looked like

Jimmy Durante in need of a shave; the smell of booze emanated from his every pore.

The church was festooned in green and red and the voices were glorious, sending the message of the angels to all us. The bum looked around the Actors Chapel in awe.

I watched him and wondered. What had brought this old wino to this pew tonight, of all nights? Stillness came upon him as the mass progressed. Then, in an instant, he turned to me, Mary, and my brother Willie, mumbled something, "It's been 50 years… since…"

Tears trickled down his boozed up old face, joyful tears. It caught me by surprise and I found myself choked up as well, the trumpets swelling behind us.

Willie shook his hand, as if they were old pals and said sincerely, "Merry Christmas."

It was a genuine Christmas moment. The angels might make messengers out of shepherds, winos, bad-tempered brothers, or bust-out actors, but it's always the same, "Peace on Earth, Good Will Towards All Men."

And a happy new year too!

CHAPTER TWELVE

2008

GLASCOTT'S

Irish American News
February 2008

A month into my 60th year of eating and drinking and I find myself running on a treadmill fighting the medicine ball of munch that hangs above my manhood. I know if I don't start working out I'll eventually explode so here I am.

My mind wanders as the tunes on my Ipod jump from Bowie to Barry White. I look up at the TVs hanging from the ceiling. It's all garbage except for football highlights, which get me moving on the mill like Devon Hester. And then I see a cable commercial that takes me back over 35 years to Glascott's Groggery.

I slow to a walk as sweat pours over my smelly trunk and pull out my earplugs. A TV commercial for Glascott's? The yuppified fern bar on the tube doesn't look like the Glascott's I knew.

But who among us looks the same as we did in 1972. The fabled Groggery has definitively had some work done. The customers in the commercial don't look like the rummies I knew from the Grog.

It still sits on the southwest corner of Webster and Halsted, probably been a saloon since Depression days. Larry Glascott Sr. was the owner and in my era his seven sons ran the pub.

The redheaded Glascott brothers had grown up in the hood over on Burling, a tough neighborhood in them days, not the Lincoln Park weenie roast it is today.

Each of the Glascotts looked like they woke up every morning and started their day with a bowl of nails for breakfast.

I was a student at the Goodman School of Drama back then, a raw actor and unshaven hipster. The Glascott brothers had started a weekly special "Penny Beer Night". That's right, beers were only a penny. I think this was designed to bring in girls and it did. It also attracted horny broke hippies like me and my pals.

I walked into Glascott's my first night and the place had a special glow. A sign in the back said, "Get Drunk and Be Somebody", and I knew I had found my new home.

Soon after discovering this friendly Irish oasis I started frequenting Glasscott's during the day. We'd have the place to ourselves, just some pals and me and five or six local alkies.

The guy who cooked burgers in the back and swept up was Paul Porter. "What's My Line" is just waitin' for him!" cracked day bartender John McCloskey.

John Terrence McCloskey took his bartending seriously. He wore a white shirt and white apron and sported a moustache and dry wit that came in handy dealing with the bar stool confessions he heard all day.

John was also from a large family of brothers, like me. He kept a volume of Shakespeare behind the bar and his literary acumen was astounding.

Many a wintry afternoon was spent at Glascott's sharing bon mots with McCloskey. When my pal Jack Whalen attempted to pass a rubber check at the bar, McCloskey told him, "There are seven Glascott brothers and each one will kill you in a different way."

We started using the side door on Webster so the boozehounds that sat in the front couldn't give us the evil eye upon our entrance each day.

When McCloskey learned I was an actor he would riffle the pages of the Bard and place a play in front of me. "Lemme hear ya do this one."

I'd wet my whistle, lift the tome to my hands and pronounce to the few, sad stalwarts on their stools, "All the worlds a stage!"

The regulars would shout for me…to shut the f…up! I believe it was at Glascott's that I realized the age-old axiom, "In order to recognize who the regulars are…you, yourself must be a regular."

Yes I was a regular at Glascott's in those days. Proud to have been one. And here I was 36 years later staring at the tube as it ran a commercial for the face-lifted tavern. As the sweat poured over my jowls I remembered the words of Willie.

To-morrow, and to-morrow, and to-morrow,
Creeps in this petty pace from day to day…
And all our yesterdays have lighted fools
The way to dusty death.
Life's but a walking shadow, a poor player,
That struts and frets his hour upon the stage.

Glascott's Groggery no longer holds the glow it did for me in my youth. But there is some consolation. I can still lift a glass and trade quips with my old pal John Terrence McCloskey, because he's been married to my sister for over 30 years.

AN IRISH UNDERTAKER'S FINALE

Irish American News
March 2008

He was the master of the graceful exit.

Andrew J. McGann Sr. had been burying the South Side Irish since 1948. Last month was our turn to bury him.

Andy's wake drew a hardy crowd of mourners to St. Catherine of Alexandria church in Oak Lawn. Photos from Andy's life were decked out along the apron of the altar, a testament to Andy's many years in politics as State Representative out of the 18th Ward and city of Chicago commissioner. As director of McGann & Son funeral home, Andy had officiated at the send-offs for all their moms and dads.

Andy was laid out in his mourning suit, starched white shirt and tie, grey gloves, and alongside him in his coffin rested the black Homburg felted hat that was his signature. Serenity suited him. He looked as though he was about to leave on a trip.

The trip began in the '40's at McGann's Tavern, his father's joint at 75th and Halsted. Roger Sheehy worked the funeral home across the street, took Andy under his wing, and taught him the business. Andy went to war twice with the Navy and Marines, raised a family, helped thousands of families in their darkest hour, and got into politics.

His wake brought generations of families he touched. Standing near the coffin, Illinois Speaker of the House Mike Madigan said, "Andy McGann was a legend…the legend developed in his role as a funeral director, but went well beyond that in terms of his personal relationships with thousands of people he met in his life. And he was clearly one of the sincerest people that ever lived. Whatever he said, he believed."

At the wake his nephew told of how Andy once claimed, "I never get hangovers. I think I actually have this ability to drink myself sober. I've never, ever in my life had a hangover."

Andy's McGann's rosy Irish face, hair of white, and twinkling eyes were without guile; tears came to him as easily as laughter. In the back of the church stood Chris Cieplak, Andy's protégé in the funeral business. He looked nervous on the eve of the funeral he would direct, one that had been planned for years over lunches with his mentor, Andy.

The morning of his funeral they came through the snow and biting cold for the send-off; senators, cops, aldermen, lobbyists, and McGaffers. Burke, Keane, O'Connell, McLaughlin, Giglio, Hynes, and Tunney. Bill Harvey, bartender at Ken's on Western Ave., was there too. His mother had always told him in hushed tones, "Nobody does it like McGann."

"Danny Boy" played on the organ while the congregation waited. And then the sound of a lone Emerald Society bagpiper playing Garryowen, signaled the approach of the casket. Four altar boys and ten priests met Andy in the middle of the aisle.

Andy loved to party and it looked like this was going to be a dignified doozy. Father Lion welcomed everyone to the "celebration of the life of

Andrew J. McGann." Andy had picked out all the readings and hymns for the funeral. He would be speaking from beyond through the scriptures.

Cook County Judge Pat McGann eulogized his uncle with love and humor, adding to the lexicon of Andy McGann stories. He finished with Andy's trademark keen, *"Come now, come Andy, come home...the flowers are appearing in the fields, the season of joyful song has come...come this is home."*

State police stopped traffic in both directions on Cicero and Central for the funeral procession to Holy Sepulchre. Hundreds of cars snaked through the snowy cemetery to the chapel for Andy's final goodbye. A Navy color guard and bugler played Taps. There wasn't a dry eye in the room.

A luncheon at the Oak Lawn Hilton followed the funeral. His pals toasted Andy and stories of his adventures were re-told. Like the time he snubbed Sinatra. Or the night he and his pals kept calling the White House to talk to their hero, Jack Kennedy, until the Secret Service showed up and told Andy to knock it off.

Another protégé of Andy's, Phil Maher, told the story of the day Andy led a funeral to the wrong cemetery. As he cruised through Mt. Olivet looking for the burial plot he realized his mistake and made a wide u-turn through the marble orchard and led the procession back out onto 111th street to Holy Sepulchre. As they exited the hearse the family hugged him and said, "Oh Andy, you took us by the graves of all our relatives, thank you, how did you know?"

I said it before; Andy McGann was the only guy who could make a dead man comfortable.

He would have been proud of Chris Cieplak and Phil Maher on his funeral day. They sent their mentor off with the same class he reserved for all of the Southside Irish. Well done, lads.

Father Lion told us at the funeral, "the angels led Andy into paradise." They are in for one hell of a good time up there. We will not see his like again.

WILLIE

Irish American News
May 2008

I was always a little bit afraid of my brother Willie. He was almost exactly ten years older than me.

I didn't see a lot of my brothers Paul or Danny growing up since they were in the seminary, but my brothers Willie, John, and Brian were posters boy for reform school. And Willie was their ringleader.

I was the baby and the perfect patsy for all their pranks.

When I was two, Willie was twelve. When I was five, he was fifteen. He invented a little stunt and taught it to my brothers. He would take his index finger, stick it in his mouth and get it soaked with saliva, and then insert the finger into your ear and swish it around. He called this a "wet nasty".

Being on the receiving end of a wet nasty was ....well, nasty.

When I was six, Willie was sixteen. Probably had been smoking for ten years by then. He was also an expert at swearing. He could string together a series of a dozen expletives at a time. Cuss words flowed from him like machine gun fire. I was impressed.

Willie was called Houli long before I claimed the name.

When I was 16, Willie got me a job on Christmas break as his runner at the Chicago Board of Trade.

I watched him in action in the pits and was impressed with his machismo as he traded. He would bring me around after the closing bell and introduce me as "my kid brother Mike."

One of the traders in the pit was a blind guy who had a Seeing Eye dog and yet somehow he managed to trade. I remarked to Billy one day on how sorry I felt for the guy and he told me, "That guy would cut your heart out and eat it if he could, don't give him a break, he's poison!"

Mister Compassion he was not.

Willie had a weakness for women, particularly beautiful but crazy chicks. Back in his high roller days of the seventies he had a girlfriend that he claimed was certifiable, call her wacky Wanda.

Wanda was a knockout, a hottie without a home. But hell hath no fury like Wacky Wanda scorned. After one of her and Willie's lovers' spats she poured gasoline over the door to his apartment and torched it.

Attorney Mike Nash lived just behind Bill in an apartment complex called Hemingway House. One morning he gets a frantic call from my brother, "You gotta come over here right away, I might need a lawyer."

Nash hurries over and finds Willie with two cops in his apartment. Beautiful Wanda has locked herself in his bathroom and refuses to leave. Willie called the cops when he couldn't get her to go.

Cop knocks on the bathroom door, "Okay Wanda, now come on, Mr. Houlihan wants you to leave."

I'm not goin' anywhere!

Come on now, Wanda, this is the police; open this door or we will break it down.

No response.

Cop says, "Are you going to come out of there and leave the premises?"

Nash says the voluptuous Wanda finally opens the door and marches right past them to stand in the middle of Willie's living room…in her birthday suit.

She puts her hands on her hips and glares at the men defiantly. Cop turns to Willie and says, "Lemme get this straight, you want HER to leave?

We told these stories and laughed at Willie's wake last month.

His journey with cancer was a rough one. He fought it and cursed it every step of the way. He took the old poem literally, Do Not Go Gentle Into that Good Night. Just ask the nurses and doctors who wrestled with him at the end and tried to subdue him during his delirium. Ask the nurse he punched… or the one he bit.

In the end, Willie saved redemption for the last. I sent my friend Fr. Dan Malette to see him about three weeks before he died.

Fearful that Willie might have thrown him out of the hospital room, I called Fr. Dan and asked him how it went.

Danny told me, "Your brother has great faith. You must have had very loving parents. We had a wonderful talk and I gave him the sacraments and anointed him."

Willie's street smarts had finally led him to salvation. Mister Lucky had cheated the devil at last.

The left-handed son of Bill and Sis Houlihan was a rogue and a rascal and we loved him for it. He's got a front row seat tonight. He's probably givin' Mother Theresa a wet nasty as we speak.

So Semper Fi, Willie, save a spot up there for the rest of us.

OLLIE O'DONNELL'S MORATORIUM

Irish American News
June 2008

"Everybody's doin' it."

That's what I told my brother when we learned he was gonna die earlier this year. I know that sounds like a harsh retort but Willie always enjoyed a sardonic quip.

Getting old sucks, everybody agrees on that. You find yourself recognizing more and more names in the Irish scratch sheet every day.

So I'm declaring a moratorium on any Hooliganism columns dealing with dead people... right after this one.

When I opened the paper last month I was shocked to see that Trish O'Connell Frawley had died suddenly. See Trish was still a young lady, the 1982 St. Patrick's Day parade queen, and I remember seeing her at plenty of Irish functions over the years.

Her ex husband Tom Frawley told me, "Tricia's pride and joy was our 11 year old daughter Mary Clare…and even though we were divorced, she was my PAL! There wasn't a day that went by that we did not speak! Quite frankly, we were better divorced than married."

That's probably true of a lot of Irish couples.

Tom is planning on organizing a tribute CD to Trish and donating proceeds to the American Heart Association with music from Joe McShane, Catherine O'Connell (her cousin), and Kathleen Keane. Watch for news on how to purchase the CD in upcoming Irish American News.

Her cousin told me, "We lost a great girl in our Trish."

It's true when they tell ya only the good die young. The Irish landscape around Chicago will be lonelier now without this beautiful flower, Patricia O'Connell Frawley. God bless you, Trish.

The young mother's passing got me to thinking of the old story of Ollie O'Donnell. Ollie was a lonely bachelor in his forties, kind of a skinny marink who kept to himself. He wasn't very remarkable in any conventional sense, certainly not handsome. He looked like a long handled frying pan.

But what put the sizzle in Ollie was his devotion to the dead. He'd been writing obituaries for years for the Southtown and ambitious corpses could only hope their lives merited an Ollie O'Donnell obit.

One day Ollie got a call from Shep Lavery, whose daughter Alice had died, leaving behind a distraught husband and three little kids. Shep was understandably upset. Alice was only in her late thirties and she had given her dad grandchildren and a great son-in-law, Murph Murphy. Shep was determined that his daughter Alice was going to get an Ollie O'Donnell obit.

Ollie had heard it all before, what a wonderful person Alice had been and how she was a great mother and a what a wonderful swimmer she was in high school. But something happened to Ollie when Shep sent over a picture of Alice. Her Irish beauty captivated the ol' frying pan as he looked over her notes. He called Shep back and said, "Tell me more about Alice."

Shep talked for hours about his daughter. He had Ollie laughing along with him when he told of her mischievous side as a kid. When Shep recounted what a wonderful mother Alice had been, tears streamed down the fryin' pan's face.

That night Ollie dreamed of the lovely Alice. In the dream he was young and they met before her marriage. She laughed at his jokes as he glided her across a dance floor in Paris. She rested her head on the frying pan's shoulder and sighed, "Oh Ollie, I wish it could always be like this."

Ollie awoke kissing his pillow. He leapt from the bed and began writing the greatest obit of his career for Alice Lavery, the woman he loved.
What appeared in the paper the next day was more mash note than memorial.

That night Ollie sat in his kitchen staring at her photo and wondered what might have been. He had never laid eyes on her but her eyes spoke to him.

Ollie opened up a bottle of Bushmills he kept above the fridge for emergencies. One ice cube and four fingers would chase these blues away. He put on a Frank Patterson record, sat back and poured his heart out to her picture.

A half hour later the picture was talking back to Ollie. Alice said, "You'll never know unless you see me in person, Ollie". The fryin' pan jumped into his black suit and headed off for the funeral home.

The line went out the door at Sheehy's but Ollie never considered bagging the wake. He stood patiently on the eario listening to more stories of the late lamented Alice Lavery.

When Ollie finally knelt at her casket he could feel the eyes of Murph Murphy burning into his back with jealousy. The fryin' pan suddenly realized that this romance wasn't going to work. Who was he kidding? She was married, with children, and on top of everything else she was dead.

Biting his lip, Ollie stood and broke for the door in embarrassment. As he slipped his coat on, an attractive young woman touched his arm and asked if he was indeed "the man from the newspaper?"

Ollie gazed into her eyes. She was a dead ringer for Alice, only younger and with larger breasts.

"Oh thank you so much for the wonderful article on my sister, I'm Evelyn Lavery."

This is where the camera pulls back, the music swells, and we roll the credits. The moratorium starts now.

INDEX